What Every Engineer
Should Know About
Human Resources Management

WHAT EVERY ENGINEER SHOULD KNOW
A Series

Editor

William H. Middendorf

Department of Electrical and Computer Engineering
University of Cincinnati
Cincinnati, Ohio

Other volumes in preparation

What Every Engineer Should Know About Human Resources Management

Desmond D. Martin
Richard L. Shell

Cincinnati, Ohio

MARCEL DEKKER, INC.
New York and Basel

Library of Congress Cataloging in Publication Data

Martin, Desmond D   [Date]
    What every engineer should know about human
resources management.

    (What every engineer should know ; v. 5)
    Includes bibliographical references and index.
    1. Personnel management. I. Shell, Richard L.,
[Date] joint author. II. Title. III. Title:
Human resources management.
HF5549.M326   658.4   80-22329
ISBN 0-8247-1130-0   *HF*
                        5549
                        .M326
                        1980

MARCEL DEKKER, INC.
270 Madison Avenue, New York, New York 10016

Current printing (last digit):
10 9 8 7 6 5 4 3 2

PRINTED IN THE UNITED STATES OF AMERICA

The authors dedicate this book to
SueAnn Shell and Nicole and James Martin

Preface

The purpose of this book is to provide technical managers with tested management concepts and techniques that can be applied to increase both managerial and organizational effectiveness. In order to achieve this goal, the analysis of management problems has been broken down to include sound principles and practices of management with a heavy emphasis on behavioral concepts.

While much has been written about management and organizational behavior in the past quarter century, the majority of that work has focused on general rather than technical management. This book is designed to contain a concise no-nonsense practical approach that will help engineering, scientific, and professional staff managers improve their managerial and leadership skills. Much of the current research in general and technical management, as well as applied behavior science knowledge, is integrated into the modern engineering and scientific environment.

The entire book emphasizes application rather than broad exploration of contrasting theories or ideas. The widespread educational, research, practical, and consulting experience of the authors has been utilized in putting the most useful management concepts into a meaningful and understandable framework. The specific chapter content has been strongly influenced by comments received from technical managers who have attended management seminars conducted by the authors throughout the United States.

Since the turn of the century more and more engineers have assumed the responsibility of managing human resources. During the past several years data available at leading universities concerning college of engineering alumni indicates that approximately two-thirds of all graduates are working at some level of management in just ten years following receipt of their bachelor degrees. Considering the importance of technology and the likely increase of scientific and technical problems that will face managers of the future, the number of engineers in management is likely to increase. Clearly, the need for this book exists and should be very helpful to practicing engineering, scientific, and professional staff managers. In addition to being used by the individual practitioner, this book is also recommended for use by colleges of business and engineering in courses that are designed to upgrade the knowledge of engineering and other technical students in the vital area of human resource management.

The authors wish to express special thanks to Dr. William H. Middendorf, Professor of Electrical Engineering, University of Cincinnati, for his support and editorial suggestions, and Dean Albert J. Simone of the College of Business Administration, University of Cincinnati, for his special facilitative effort. In fact, the help of these two colleagues was instrumental in making this book a reality. Dr. Stephen Green, Associate Professor of Management, University of Cincinnati, offered considerable encouragement throughout this project. The authors' thanks would not be complete without mentioning the magnanimous typing effort performed by Ms. Rhonda Christman and Ms. Linda Wefer of the Department of Mechanical and Industrial Engineering, University of Cincinnati.

Desmond D. Martin
Richard L. Shell

Contents

About the Authors

Desmond D. Martin is Professor of Management in the College of Business Administration at the University of Cincinnati. He has extensive consulting experience with major organizations, both public and private, including American Standard, American Crystal Sugar Company, Scovill Corporation, U. S. Department of Labor, U. S. Army Corps of Engineers, and the U. S. Environmental Protection Agency. He conducts seminars throughout the United States on important management topics, and has published numerous articles on management development techniques and motivation. He received his B.A. degree (1959) from Michigan State University, his M.S. degree (1961) from Florida State University, and his D.B.A. degree (1964) from Michigan State University. He is a member of the Academy of Management.

Richard L. Shell is Professor of Industrial Engineering in the College of Engineering at the University of Cincinnati. Previously he was Professor and Head of the Department of Management in the College of Business Administration at the University of Cincinnati. He has held engineering and management positions with Bourns, Ampex, and IBM, and has served as an engineering and management consultant for government and private industry. He is presently serving as a member of the board of directors for several corporations. In 1978 Professor Shell received the American Institute of Industrial Engineers Phil Carroll Award for outstanding achievement in work measurement and methods engineering, and in 1980 he received the University of Cincinnati George B. Barbour Award for outstanding service in teaching and for the development of student-faculty relations. Professor Shell's research interests include technical administration, manufacturing engineering, productivity measurement and improvement, and word processing and data processing. He has published widely in these and other fields. He received his B.S.M.E. degree (1961) from the University of Iowa, his

M.S.M.E. degree (1963) from the University of Kentucky, and his Ph.D. degree (1970) from the University of Illinois. He is a registered professional engineer in Ohio and Kentucky. Professor Shell is a member of the American Institute of Industrial Engineers and the Society of Manufacturing Engineers, among other professional societies.

What Every Engineer
Should Know About
Human Resources Management

1

Introduction

Management Defined

Management may be defined as the establishment and realization of goals through the cooperative efforts of all concerned persons. To further explain this definition, additional discussion is useful. The word *goals* usually implies the collective goals of the organization and certain personal goals of participating individuals. Both types of goal realization are required for organizational success. The term *cooperative efforts* implies that management must be able to obtain the cooperation of persons, and direct their efforts toward goal realization. Management must also be able to measure, evaluate, and control the efforts of all persons within the organization. In addition to individuals within the organization, the term *concerned persons* means that management must be able to properly interface and benefit from individuals outside of the organization that bear influence on ultimate goal realization. Indeed, management is complex in its structure and activities. It consists of people and physical things. Consequently, the key to successful management for engineers and professional staff is obtaining the proper balance between the theory, principles, and practices of management, and human behavior in organizations. It may be said, *the world is management.*

Management: An Art and Science

Is management an art? Is management a science? Considerable opinion has been set forth concerning the answer to these questions without definitive agreement. An examination of the fundamentals of science and art will be helpful in the understanding of management.

Science relates to knowledge developed from experimentation conducted to determine underlying principles. Commonly, this development of knowledge

1

involves physical experimentation or empirical observation to generate, classify, and analyze data, and formulate statistically valid conclusions. Berelson and Steiner have summarized the important characteristics of science in the outline below:[1]

1. The procedures are public: There is made available to the scientific community a minutely detailed description of the procedures and findings.
2. The definitions are precise: Each important term is clearly delineated, so that common meanings can be universally applied.
3. The data collecting is objective: Regardless of whether data confirm or refute hypotheses or personal preferences, they are accurately measured and treated without bias.
4. The findings must be replicable: Other scientists must be able to reproduce the study and reach the same finding before a hypothesis is generally accepted as validated.
5. The approach is systematic and cumulative: Ultimately the goal is to construct an organized system of verified propositions, a body of theory; individual research projects should be related to existing theory to achieve an overall theoretical structure; new studies may be indicated by gaps or apparent inconsistencies among findings.
6. The purposes are explanation, understanding, and prediction; the growth of understanding and certainty, the decisions concerning control, creation, or change of conditions are applications of a science; they become part of the science only as they assist in meeting the six criteria discussed herein.

While it is unlikely that management will ever exactly match the characteristics of science, it appears that more science is being incorporated into the ongoing practice of management. A possible reason for this trend is the ever-increasing complexity of most business operations. The scientific approach helps solve management problems relating to government regulations, energy availability, productivity enhancement, environmental requirements, technology development, computerization, and cost control, just to mention a few.

Art is defined by Webster as "skill in performance acquired by experience, study, or observation." By this definition a large part of management can be classified as an art. Certainly it is true that managers are many times evaluated on their skill in performance, and managers enhance that skill by experience, study, and observation.

It can be concluded that for most organizations, management today should be a combination of art and science. Management should be a mixture of scientific method and analytical techniques, integrated with intuition and judgment derived from experience. In most situations, this combination is necessary to effectively manage change constantly occurring within the organization.

Management Theory and Thought

Management can be further explained and better understood by reviewing the major theory and thought approaches developed over the past several decades. Practicing managers and researchers have developed their own views and ideas about management. In some cases overlay and similarity has occurred, causing reinforcement, while at other times a totally different concept was created. This development of different "schools" of management was apparent a number of years ago and has been summarized by Harold Koontz as follows:

> There are the behaviorists . . . who see management as a complex of the interpersonal relationships and the basis of management theory the tentative tenets of the new and undeveloped science of psychology. There are also those who see management theory as simply a manifestation of the institutional and cultural aspects of sociology. Still others, observing the central core of management is the decision making, branch in all directions from this core to encompass everything in organization life. Then, there are mathematicians who think of management primarily as an exercise in logical relationships expressed in symbols and the omnipresent and ever revered model. But the entanglement of growth reaches its ultimate when the study of management is regarded as one of a number of systems and subsystems, with an understandable tendency for the researcher to be dissatisfied until he has encompassed the entire physical and cultural universe as a management system.[2]

The subsections that follow briefly summarize the thought and theory of the major management schools.

Scientific Management

The first structured school of management theory and thought, defined as *scientific management*, evolved from the industrial revolution. An early developer of scientific management was Frederick W. Taylor in his work at Midvale Steel Company during the late nineteenth century.[3] He believed that management should define specific tasks for every worker to complete in a specified time, select the worker best suited for each task, and be concerned with worker motivation. In short, he believed that management should solve problems with logical study and scientific research as opposed to relying on rules of thumb and trial and error methods.

A number of others worked to enlarge the practice of scientific management. Henry L. Gantt, an associate of Taylor, worked to improve the scheduling of manufacturing operations, and Frank B. and Lillian E. Gilbreth developed techniques for studying human motions and improving methods (micromotion study).[4] In addition to time study and methods analysis, the early scientific management school fostered several useful and commonly accepted industrial practices including job evaluation, worker training, and personnel and industrial relations.

Process/Functional Management

The management process school or functional management treats management more as a profession than does probably any other school of management. This theory states that the basic management function is consistent, independent of the nature of the organization. The theory assumes that once the manager's functions have been defined, knowledge of practical methods of implementing these functions can be systematically observed, evaluated, and taught. A practitioner can apply this theory much as an engineer might use a book of mathematical tables as a reference.

The beginning of functional management was initiated by a French engineer, Henry J. Fayol, who in 1861 published *Administration industrielle et generale*. This book was not published in the United States until 1949.[5] Based on his own career, Fayol observed that all industrial activities could be grouped into the following six major categories:

Technical
Commercial
Financial
Security
Accounting
Managerial

The first five categories were relatively well known and encompassed the activities of manufacturing, buying, selling, and record keeping. Consequently, Fayol was most concerned with managerial activities and formulated a number of general principles relating to authority, responsibility, division of work, remuneration, centralization, discipline, and unity of command.

A number of other authors helped structure functional management. These included Mooney and Reiley[6] and Dennison[7] for their work in organization, and Tread[8] for his work in leadership.

Another early proponent of the management process theory, Davis, proposed three organic functions of a manager as follows:[9]

Planning: The exercise of creative thinking in the solution of business problems. It involves the determination of what is to be done, how and where
it is to be done, and who shall be responsible.

Organizing: The process of creating and maintaining the requisite conditions
for the effective and economical execution of plans. These conditions are
principally concerned with morale, organizational structure, procedure,
and the various physical factors of performance.

Controlling: The regulation of business activities in accordance with the
requirements of business plans. The control process included three principal phases: (a) The assurance of proper performance as specified by the
plan; (b) the coordination of effort in conformity with the requirement
of the plan; (c) the removal of interferences with proper execution of the
plan.

More contemporary supporters of the management process theory include
Koontz and O'Donnell,[10] Terry,[11] and Dale.[12] They have noted activities such
as leading, activating, motivating, staffing, and influencing others as individual
management functions.

Human Relations

The practice of scientific management during the 1920s and 1930s, while
successful in fulfilling workers' economic needs, failed to consider psychological
needs. Much of the early work in industrial psychology was based on a book by
Lillian Gilbreth.[13] The first major study to examine the psychological factors
relating to worker productivity was the Hawthorne experiments conducted by
Mayo and Roethlisberger.[14] The most interesting results of this study was that
worker output increased no matter what change was made in physical conditions, e.g., noise or lighting levels. The fact that the workers perceived they were
a "select" group and were under observation caused increased output. In short,
the psychological factors outweighed the physical environment considerations.

More recent contemporaries in the human relations field include Keith
Davis[15] and William Scott.[16] Human relations knowledge added to scientific
management and functional management theories and thought, but there were
still shortcomings—the more complete understanding of human behavior. While
the detailed topics relating to behavior in organizations are discussed in later
chapters, a brief overview of the behavioral science school of management
follows.

Behavioral Science

A number of persons have contributed to the theory and thought of behavior
as it relates to management. These include Maslow,[17] Bakke,[18] Dalton,[19]

Stogdell,[20] Likert,[21] Sayles,[22] Leavitt,[23] Vroom,[24] Herzberg,[25] Argyris,[26] McGregor,[27] and Bennis.[28] These behaviorists focus on the development of individual and group needs, and the interaction of these needs with the organizational environment. When this approach is integrated into the broader "socio-technical" system, it has become widely recognized as an important part of the effective management of scientists and engineers. One of the major purposes of this book is to provide engineering and scientific managers with proven managerial and applied behavioral tools that will help increase the effectiveness of their ogranizational units.

Social Systems

The social system approach views workers from a much less flexible viewpoint than the behavioral theorist. Where as in behavioral science, motivation is contingent upon each worker's needs and aspirations, the social system theorist relates more to basic motivators relevant to the present culture. The social system school looks at a corporation as basically an input-output model, with the employees working only when they feel the inducements received equal or outweigh their contributions.

March and Simon[29] and Simon and coworkers[30] have outlined the major characteristics of an organization following the input-output model:

1. An organization is a system of interrelated social behaviors of a number of persons whom we shall call the participants in the organization.
2. Each participant and each group of participants receives from the organization inducements, in return for which he or she makes contributions to the organization.
3. Each participant will continue his or her participation in an organization only so long as the inducements offered him are as great or greater (measured in terms of his values and in terms of the alternatives open to him) than the contributions he is asked to make.
4. The contributions provided by the various groups of participants are the source from which the organization manufactures the inducements offered to the participants.
5. Hence, an organization is "solvent"—and will continue in existence—only so long as contributions are sufficient to provide inducements in large enough measure to draw forth these contributions.

Management Science

The management science approach has also been defined as the mathematical school, the decision theory school, quantitative methods, and operations research. The modern day foundation for management science began during World War II when mathematical models were developed to solve problems relating to the management of war operations. Since that time contributing management science authors have included Morse and Kimball,[31] Churchman, Ackoff, and Arnoff,[32] Miller and Starr,[33] Bierman, Fouraker, and Jaedicke,[34] Teichroew,[35] Wagner,[36] and Hicks.[37]

The mathematical school attempts to approach each management situation with a parallel mathematic model (either deterministic or probabilistic). The problem is then solved using the precise logical structure of mathematics. If the model does indeed match the business problem at hand and the computations can be completed, the mathematical approach has value. Recent developments in computer technology have increased the usefulness of this approach. With faster processing capabilities and larger storage, large masses of data can be input and processed to yield problem solutions.[38]

The decision-making process has probably received more attention than any other subject among management scientists. Traditional decision theory stresses rational thinking, the acquisition of valid data, and quantitative models to arrive at a proper decision. Examples of different business situations may be developed to produce several alternate solutions to a particular problem. There is also an emphasis on objectivity in evaluating different alternatives.

Systems and Contingency

Management has borrowed the systems concept from the physical and natural sciences. This approach requires the interrelatedness of all activities within an organization. Norbert Weiner contributed much theory and thought to modern day systems concepts.[39] An early pioneer in applying systems concepts to management was Kenneth Boulding.[40] A number of other authors helped foster the systems viewpoint in management including Johnson, Kast, and Rosengweig,[41] Churchman,[42] Bellman,[43] and Cleland and King.[44]

The contingency approach came into being because of the individual short-comings of previously developed schools of management. For example, the behavioral approach works well in many situations involving people problems, but it does not produce results in operations problems requiring the techniques of management science for solution. Similar statements could be made concerning the other management schools. The first authors to observe the need for a contingency approach included Woodward,[45] Fiedler,[46] and Lorsch and Lawrence.[47]

The contingency approach requires that the practice and application of management theory should be contingent upon the needs of a specific management situation. Consequently, behavioral and scientific techniques should be applied along with selected principles and practices from each school of management to solve existing problems. The successful manager must have the ability to recognize which management approach(es) to use in a given situation at a particular point in time.

Emphasis of This Book

This book addresses two major aspects of management. The first is what engineering, scientific, and professional staff should know about the principles and practices of effective management. The second is what that staff should know about behavior in organizations. Many authorities on engineering and professional management believe that a knowledge of these two areas is necessary for the attainment of managerial effectiveness.

Principles and Practice

Following the definition of "management," this first chapter has discussed the "art" and "science" components of management. A brief overview of the schools of management has provided the reader with an understanding of the important theories and thought of management, and a number of references that explain in detail the beginning of modern day management. Finally, the concept of "contingency" or "situational" management was offered as the approach to be used by engineers and professional staff.

Chapter 2 is devoted to planning and forecasting. Effective and efficient management must begin with planning, and to plan one must be able to forecast the future. Aspects of long-range and operational (short-term) planning are discussed. In addition, a number of commonly used forecasting techniques are reviewed.

Chapter 3 addresses the management functions of organizing and staffing. An historical background is included to give the reader a prospective on how and why today's organizations came into being. The principles of "unity of command" and "division of labor" are discussed. The proper roles for line and staff are identified. Span of management concepts are defined along with the methodology necessary for correct organizational design. The final section of the chapter provides insight into the importance and nature of good employee selection.

Chapter 4 highlights the principles of directing and controlling. Responsibility and authority are discussed and suggestions for delegation are offered. Ideas for salary administration and performance measurement are important management concerns. The relationship of budgets to control is reviewed along with management information systems. Finally, suggestions are offered for the application of critical path scheduling to enhance project direction and control.

Chapter 5 is devoted to the important management activity of decision making. The nature of the decision-making process is summarized, followed by a recommended systems analysis technique to aid decision making. In addition, the concepts of "utility theory" and "expected value" are discussed as they relate to decision making.

Behavior in Organizations

Chapter 6 contains a concise development of the emergence and importance of individual and group needs. An understanding of these needs is the cornerstone of modern behavioral management, and the significant impact of individual needs on group development and organizational effectiveness is covered. Specific attention is given to the needs of engineering and scientific personnel, and what the unique nature of these needs means to the modern technical manager.

Chapter 7 analyzes the number one management problem, namely, building effective communications within the engineering and scientific environment. The major types and dimensions of organizational communication are classified. The importance of informal and nonverbal communication is dealt with in a practical context. Several techniques and tools to improve the level of understanding within the engineering and scientific environment are provided. Attention is given to major problem areas including tips on overcoming defensiveness, increasing communication feedback and participation, and building an overall organization climate that is characterized by mutual trust.

Chapter 8 focuses on the modern motivational problems that face managers of engineering, scientific, and professional employees. These managers are encouraged to confront the motivation problem directly, and six basic steps are outlined that will help to make this confrontation successful. The most practical motivation models are identified and explained and are specifically put in the technical environment. The overall emphasis of this chapter is to provide a basic no-nonsense approach to motivating engineers, scientists, and professional staff.

Chapter 9 emphasizes the importance of strong leadership in effective management. Four basic leadership styles are developed and criteria are provided for choosing an appropriate style. Common leadership problems such as delegation, participation, and the facilitative role of the manager are discussed in a simple and practical manner.

Chapter 10 deals with the complex problem of organizational change. Three phases of change that are related to managerial effectiveness are explained. An analysis is made of the factors that lead to resistance to change. Since resistance to change often leads to reduced motivation, it can be an extremely costly management problem. Several tips are provided on how the engineering, scientific, and professional staff manager can properly implement change and alleviate resistance. While employee participation is often very useful in reducing resistance, it sometimes is either inappropriate or insufficient, and in these latter cases alternatives are suggested.

Chapter 11 briefly explains the popular and useful management tool known as *management by objectives* or MBO. Once the nature and purpose of MBO is clearly explained, its applicability to the engineering, scientific, and professional staff environment is examined. Management by objectives can increase control, improve performance appraisals, enhance interpersonal communication, reduce resistance to change, and raise the motivational levels within the units where it is properly implemented. This chapter provides specific insight into how technical managers can install an MBO system in their organizational units.

Chapter 12 summarizes the impact of the major managerial factors covered throughout the book on organizational effectiveness. Comments are included concerning the changing attitudes and values of the American work force and career development in the professional organization. The closing discussion centers on the future of engineering and technical management.

Notes

1. B. Berelson and G. A. Steiner, *Human Behavior,* Harcourt, Brace & World, New York, 1964, pp. 16-17.
2. H. Koontz, The Management Theory Jungle. *Academy of Management Journal,* vol. IV, no. 3, December 1961, pp. 174-175.
3. F. W. Taylor, *The Principles of Scientific Management,* Harper & Brothers, New York, 1911.
4. F. B. Gilbreth and L. E. Gilbreth, *Applied Motion Study,* Macmillan, New York, 1917.
5. H. J. Fayol, *General and Industrial Administration,* Sir Isaac Pitman & Sons, London, 1949.
6. J. D. Mooney and A. C. Reiley, *Onward Industry,* Harper & Brothers, New York, 1931; and *The Principles of Organization,* Harper & Brothers, New York, 1939.
7. H. Dennison, *Organization Engineering,* McGraw-Hill, New York, 1931.
8. O. Tread, *The Art of Leadership,* McGraw-Hill, New York, 1935.
9. R. C. Davis, *Industrial Organization and Management,* Harper & Brothers, New York, 1940, pp. 35-36.
10. H. Koontz and C. O'Donnell, *Management: A Systems and Contingency Analysis of Managerial Functions,* 6th ed., McGraw-Hill, New York, 1976.
11. G. Terry, *Principles of Management,* 6th ed., Irwin, Homewood, Ill., 1972.
12. E. Dale, *Management Theory and Practice,* 3rd ed., McGraw-Hill, New York, 1973.
13. L. M. Gilbreth, *The Psychology of Management,* Macmillan, New York, 1914.
14. E. Mayo, *The Human Relations of an Industrial Civilization,* Harvard University Press, Cambridge, Mass., 1933.
15. K. Davis, *Human Relations in Business,* McGraw-Hill, New York, 1954.
16. W. G. Scott, Modern Human Relations in Perspective. *Personnel Administration,* vol. 22, no. 6, 1959.
17. A. Maslow, *Motivation and Personality,* Harper & Brothers, New York, 1954.

18. E. W. Bakke, *Bonds of Organization,* Harper & Row, New York, 1950.
19. M. Dalton, *Men Who Manage,* John Wiley & Sons, New York, 1959.
20. R. M. Stogdell, *Individual Behavior and Group Achievement,* Oxford University Press, London, 1959.
21. R. Likert, *New Patterns of Management,* McGraw-Hill, New York, 1961.
22. L. Sayles, *Managerial Behavior,* McGraw-Hill, New York, 1964.
23. H. J. Leavitt, *Managerial Psychology,* University of Chicago Press, Chicago, 1964.
24. V. H. Vroom, *Work and Motivation,* John Wiley & Sons, New York, 1964.
25. F. Herzberg, *Work and the Nature of Man,* World Publishing Co., Cleveland, 1966.
26. C. Argyris, *Integrating the Individual and the Organization,* John Wiley & Sons, New York, 1964.
27. D. McGregor, *The Human Side of Enterprise,* McGraw-Hill, New York, 1960.
28. W. Bennis, *Changing Organizations,* McGraw-Hill, New York, 1966.
29. J. G. March and H. A. Simon, *Organizations,* John Wiley & Sons, New York, 1958.
30. H. A. Simon, W. Smithburg, and V. A. Thompson, *Public Administration,* Alfred A. Knopf, New York, 1950.
31. P. M. Morse and G. E. Kimball, *Methods of Operations Research,* John Wiley & Sons, New York, 1951.
32. G. W. Churchman, R. L. Ackoff, and E. L. Arnoff, *Introduction to Operations Research,* John Wiley & Sons, New York, 1957.
33. D. W. Miller and M. K. Starr, *Executive Decisions and Operations Research,* Prentice-Hall, Englewood Cliffs, N.J., 1960.
34. H. Bierman, L. E. Fouraker, and R. K. Jaedicke, *Quantitative Analysis for Business Decisions,* Irwin, Homewood, Ill., 1961.
35. D. Teichroew, *An Introduction to Management Science,* John Wiley & Sons, New York, 1964.
36. H. M. Wagner, *Principles of Management Science,* Prentice-Hall, Englewood Cliffs, N.J., 1975.
37. P. E. Hicks, *Introduction to Industrial Engineering and Management Science,* McGraw-Hill, New York, 1977.
38. R. L. Shell, "Data Processing/Computers and Future Technology," *Proceedings, Tenth Annual Conference, American Technical Education Association,* October 1976.
39. N. Weiner, *Cybernetics,* The MIT Press, Cambridge, Mass., 1948.
40. K. Boulding, General Systems Theory: The Skeleton of Science. *Management Science,* April 1956.
41. R. A. Johnson, F. E. Kast, and J. E. Rosengweig, *The Theory and Management of Systems,* McGraw-Hill, New York, 1963.
42. C. W. Churchman, *The Systems Approach,* Delacorte Press, New York, 1968.
43. R. Bellman, Control Theory. *Scientific American,* vol. 211, no. 3, September 1964.

44. D. I. Cleland and W. R. King, *Systems Analysis and Project Management,* 2nd ed., McGraw-Hill, New York, 1968, 1975.
45. J. Woodward, *Industrial Organization,* Oxford University Press, London, 1965.
46. F. E. Fiedler, *A Theory of Leadership Effectiveness,* McGraw-Hill, New York, 1967.
47. J. W. Lorsch and P. R. Lawrence, *Studies in Organizational Design,* Irwin-Dorsey, Homewood, Ill., 1970.

2
Planning and Forecasting

Introduction

Planning can be viewed as a method of determining desirable future conditions and then setting goals and objectives to obtain this desired state. Typical questions that must be answered by the planner include the following: *What business are we in? What business should we be in? Who are our customers? What customers should be sought? What products or services should be added?* These are just a few of the many questions that must be answered. The humorous side of planning and forecasting was best summed up by Mark Twain who said, "Get your facts first and then you can distort them as you please."[1]

Historically, the most formal planning efforts focused upon tactical or operational type problems. Strategic or long-range planning was accomplished using intuitive approaches common with entrepreneurs. A study reported within the last 5 years shows that 63 out of 111 corporate planners surveyed were first incumbents in their position. Further, of the 48 who were not, 34 had but one predecessor.[2] Today's methods of long-range planning indicate a much more formal approach to developing and mapping out the firm's future.

Long-range Planning

Long-range planning is one of the more difficult tasks corporate executives must perform. Not only are they asked to plan a course for the firm to follow in an uncertain future, they also must forecast technology and economic conditions, as well as the social and political environments outside the firm. In addition to all of these, responsibility for a long-range plan is enormous—the survival of the corporation is totally dependent on the long-range plan. For this reason, long-range planning must be the responsibility of top management and receive high priority in the organization.

Although formal long-range planning is relatively new in the field of management, more than 80 percent of the large corporations in the United States have some kind of long-range planning. Growth objectives, technological innovation, and severe competition necessitate planning. The requirements for obtaining lead time also demands that firms make decisions long before the real need exists to fill vacant areas or implement necessary change. In a survey conducted by Toyohiro Kono, a better allocation of resources proved another important reason for long-range planning among U.S. firms.[3]

The planning process in the organization may be classified into three types: Bottom-up, top-down, and interactive. The distinction between the types relates to where the plan is presented, reviewed, and decided.

The bottom-up approach requires the operating unit or division to gather information and set goals. Planning for this approach is decentralized and corporate planning departments are relatively small. Only high level key long-range planning is made at the corporate level. Many larger U.S. firms use this type of planning.

The top-down approach, as opposed to bottom-up, has all planning done at the corporate level. Divisions are assigned goals and guidelines to follow. Large corporate planning offices are required.

Interactive planning is a cross between the bottom-up and top-down approach. There is interaction between top management and the operating unit or division. The planning department functions to gather information which it submits to top management. They then develop goals and broad directives. These are submitted to the divisions or units which then devise guidelines and formulate direct goals. The interactive approach is recommended for the greatest long-range planning effectiveness.

Sound forecasting techniques are essential to successful planning. Most companies use a number of techniques to accomplish long-range planning. In a study done in the early seventies sampling 40 firms, the median number of techniques used was four. Simulation, correlational analysis, present worth, and risk analysis were most often cited as the techniques used by these companies over a 10-year period beginning in 1959.[4] Yet another survey completed in 1978 sampling 42 companies reported that regression and concensus techniques did poorly in predicting in excess of 2 years (long-term) (Shell, unpublished results). Clearly, there exists a need for improved forecasting techniques for long-range planning.

Operational Planning

Operational plans are usually more narrow in scope than long-range plans and short term in their impact. An operational plan is often used by lower and middle level managers because they are more familiar with the plan's functions and operations. Also, the responsibilities are fewer. An operational plan will not have the overall effect on a company as will a long-term plan.

Questions addressed by an operational planner are more restrictive and specialized than those of the long-range planner. Examples of these questions might be: How many and what skill type of engineering personnel are required for a product development? What inventory levels should be maintained? What replacement policy should be used with regard to a certain type of equipment? How much of a product should be produced over a period of a year or 6 months' time? What level of tooling and test equipment should be designed to support planned production? Since the planning period is short, present trends and market position are often assumed to be relatively unchanged; thus, operational planning lends itself to the use of past data. Comparatively little forecasting is done before preparing an operational plan. Mathematical models, exponential smoothing, and the program evaluation and review technique (PERT) are frequently used for short-range planning.[5] These techniques will be discussed in later chapters. All of these techniques rely to some degree on past data.

In general, a short-term plan should be completed concurrent with long-term planning. For example, if an organization has a 1-year time horizon for operational planning and a 5-year period for long-range planning, the operational plan becomes the first year of the long-range plan. Independent of the planning horizon time period, it is recommended that both operational and long-range planning be updated at least annually. Following initial planning efforts, a long-range plan only requires complete planning for the last year, with the other years being appropriately updated. At the very least, goals established in short-term planning should be set to enhance the long-term goals. If a tight linkage exists between the long-range and operational planning, it will make long-range planning seem more action oriented and more credible to the members of the organization. Tight linkage does have a negative side; it often hinders creativity and is likely to cause managers to avoid risks. Future-oriented companies will often want a loose linkage, while consecutive cash-generating firms will choose the former.[6]

Basic Forecasting Methods

As mentioned earlier, most firms use more than one method of forecasting in both long-range and short-range planning. The variety of methods are extensive. Methods used mainly for operational planning differ from those used for long-range planning because of the uncertainty involved in predicting farther into the future. Selection of the right technique can be almost as important as the planning itself. Use of the wrong method, insufficient or incorrect data collection, or improper analysis may leave the planner and top management with a very poor prediction about the future.

Forecasting for planning is concerned with all aspects of descriptive statistics including methods for collecting, organizing, analyzing, summarizing, and presenting data, in addition to formulating valid conclusions. In a more narrow sense, the term *statistics* denotes only the data or the numerical solutions of the data, e.g., calculations of means and standard deviations. Planning is concerned with making reasonable decisions or arriving at meaninful conclusions on the basis of analysis of the forecasting data. A number of commonly used deterministic and probabilistic forecasting methods are briefly discussion in the sections that follow. These methods are included to remind readers with forecasting experience of the commonly used techniques, and to suggest that readers with minimum forecasting background consult a basic forecasting test to become familiar with the fundamental techniques.

Linear Regression

The least-squares method is commonly used to fit a straight line through a group of data points. The principle of least squares requires that if a dependent variable y is a linear function of an independent variable x, the best location of the line y = a + bx will exist when the sum of the squares of deviations of all data points from that location is minimized. The values of a and b may be obtained by solving the normal equations:

$$a = \frac{\Sigma x^2 \, \Sigma y - \Sigma x \Sigma xy}{n \Sigma x^2 - (\Sigma x)^2}$$

and

$$b = \frac{n \Sigma xy - \Sigma x \Sigma y}{n \Sigma x^2 - (\Sigma x)^2}$$

Forecasting commonly requires that the independent variable x is time. A regression line or curve y on x is often termed a trend line in time-series forecasting.

The method of least squares permits the computation of sampling errors and provides for the determination of the estimates' reliability. Confidence limits can be determined by computing the variance of y from the estimated value of y by the regression line with the following equations:

$$S_y^2 = \frac{\Sigma \epsilon_i^2}{v}$$

where

S_y^2 = confidence interval

ϵ_i^2 = square of the deviation

$= y_i - (a + bx_i)$

v = degrees of freedom

Additional confidence limits and significance tests may be determined for the regression equation depending on the forecast requirements.

For two or more independent variables, multiple linear regression may be used as expressed by the following equation:

$$y = a + b_1 x_1 + b_2 x_2 + \cdots + b_m x_m$$

where

a = a constant

b_i = partial regression coefficients

Single or multiple independent variable linear regression requires the following assumptions:

1. The regression of y on x_i is linear.
2. The data are taken from a representative forecasting population.
3. There are no extraneous variables.
4. The deviations from y are mutually independent and have the same variance for any value of x_i.
5. The deviations are normally distributed.

Curvilinear Regression and Curve Fitting

Many situations in the planning process require forecasting from nonlinear data. Calculations for nonlinear regression are best performed with computerized assistance. The following are examples of curvilinear relationships useful in forecasting for planning:

Exponential or logarithmic: $\quad y = ax^b$

Semilogarithmic: $\quad y = ae^{bx}$

Reciprocal y: $\quad y = \dfrac{1}{a + bx}$

Reciprocal x: $\quad y = a + \dfrac{b}{x}$

Hyperbolic: $\quad y = \dfrac{x}{a + bx}$

Polynomial: $\quad y = a + b_1 x + b_2 x^2 + \cdots + b_m x^m$

A number of nonlinear relationships may be transformed to linear expressions. For example, nonlinear data points following the exponential form, $y =$

ax^b, on Cartesian coordinates may be transformed to a linear relationship on logarithmic coordinates with the following equation:

$$\log y = \log a + b \log x$$

All of these functions can be statistically evaluated for their fit to the data. Commonly used measures include the standard error of y, correlation coefficient, and confidence limits.

Correlation

For linear regression, the coefficient of correlation explains how well the variables are satisfied by a given relationship. Figure 2.1 depicts data point diagrams with associated values of correlation. The correlation coefficient, r, may be computed as shown below:

$$r = \frac{n\Sigma xy - \Sigma x \Sigma y}{[n\Sigma x^2 - (\Sigma x)^2][n\Sigma y^2 - (\Sigma y)^2]^{\frac{1}{2}}}$$

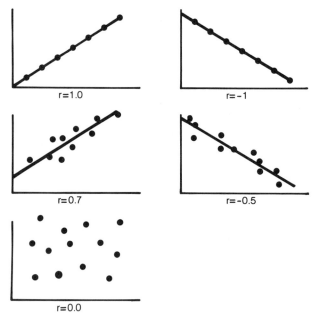

Figure 2.1 Data point diagrams with associated values of correlation coefficient

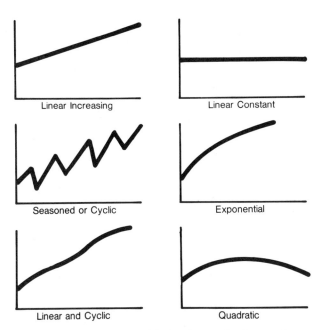

Figure 2.2 Common models for time-series forecasting

The value of r must be in the range $0 \leqslant |r| \leqslant 1$. The magnitude of the correlation coefficient indicates the strength of the relationship between variables. It should be noted that the correlation coefficient is a measure of relationship strength and is purely mathematical. It does not determine any cause or effect implications.

Moving Averages and Exponential Smoothing

Most forecasting requirements for planning are concerned with time-series data and projections. Figure 2.2 depicts examples of commonly encountered time-series models. If the planner assumes the forecast should place equal weight on all past data points, then the moving average, A_m, may be computed with the following equation:

$$A_m = \frac{x_t + x_{t-1} + \cdots + x_{t-n+1}}{n}$$

If the forecast should reflect historical data and current trends, the exponential smoothing function is recommended. This function may be expressed as follows:

$$S_t(x) = \alpha x_t + (1 - \alpha) S_{t-1}(x)$$

where

$S_t(x)$ = smoothed value of the function

α = smoothing constant

The value of the smoothing constant must lie between $0 \leqslant \alpha \leqslant 1$. When the value of the smoothing constant is small, the function $S_t(x)$ is strongly influenced by past data. When the value of the smoothing constant is large, $S_t(x)$ is influenced mostly by the current trend. It is recommended that smoothing constant values be developed from experience for specific planning and forecasting requirements.

Simulation

Up to this point, several deterministic methods of forecasting have been reviewed. In addition to these methods, certain probabilistic methods are useful.

Simulation techniques are generally used with longer-term forecasting. This is because they frequently require a great deal of time and effort to develop. A model must be created that represents a situation which will react the way a real system would. Various input is fed into the model which produces an output modeling the outcome of the real situation. Managers should use these models to answer "what if" questions that develop in many planning situations.[7]

Another modeling approach useful in planning is the Monte Carlo technique. This technique uses random variables selected from a probability distribution to input into the model. Output from this type of model is in the form of a distribution of the end results. From this, a manager can determine the most likely end result and decide whether it is acceptable.

Cost and Activity Indexes

In addition to internal data, most forecasts for planning should consider outside factors. Index numbers have been used in planning for a long time. For example, in the mid eighteenth century, an Italian, G. R. Carli, developed an index to evaluate the effects of the discovery of America on the purchasing power of money in Europe.[8] During more recent years, numerous indexes have been developed. Examples of these include wholesale and retail prices, productivity, wages, and building construction. In addition to their main point of concern, most indexes apply to a time and place, namely, a given year for a certain geographic region.

Summary

Problems of planning that face organizations today are probably more complex than ever before. In the midst of inflation, recession, unemployment, business failures, rapidly changing technologies, and political upheaval, the activity of corporate planning becomes excessively difficult. Without planning and forecasting, a firm's chance of survival becomes questionable if not improbable. It is important that engineering, scientific, and professional staff managers realize that planning serves to give an organization guidelines to follow and a standard to gauge its progress.

Notes

1. Mark Twain, quoted in Phillip F. Oswald, *Cost Estimating for Engineering and Management,* Prentice-Hall, Englewood Cliffs, N.J., 1974, p. 121.

2. James K. Brown, *Planning and the Corporate Planning Director,* The Conference Board, Washington, D.C., 1974.

3. Kono Toyohiro, Long Range Planning, Japan-U.S.A., A Comparative Study. *Long Range Planning,* October 1976.

4. Ernest C. Miller, *Advanced Techniques for Strategic Planning,* American Management Association, New York, 1971.

5. B. Render and R. L. Shell, "Forecasting Techniques for Production Planning and Control," *Proceedings, Annual Systems Engineering Conference, American Institute of Industrial Engineers,* 1975, pp. 279-303.

6. Elliot Jones, *Economic Forecasting and Corporate Planning,* The Conference Board, Washington, D.C., 1973.

7. R. L. Shell and S. Chandra, "Simulation for Automated Job-Shop Development," *Proceedings, Annual Systems Engineering Conference, American Institute of Industrial Engineers,* 1975, pp. 16-25.

8. Oswald, *Cost Estimating for Engineering and Management,* p. 148.

3

Organizing and Staffing

Historical Background

In general, an organization may be defined as a social invention developed by persons to accomplish things otherwise not possible. It is a social invention that takes a variety of people, knowledge, materials, and equipment and gives them structure and purpose to become an interrelated effective unit with common goals. An organization may also be described as a structured system by which decisions are transmitted from management to subordinate levels, taking into account communication, influence, authority, responsibility, and loyalty. Staffing supplies the people to operate the enterprise through the organizational structure.

Why have organized structure? In today's economic environment things are constantly changing; therefore, it becomes necessary for an organization to be flexible enough to identify the need for change, and through internal manipulation make the change as smoothly as possible. In essence, organizational structure is a tool of effectiveness, and if organizations were more effective without it, it would not be needed. But as organizations increase in size, structure becomes necessary for both efficiency and effectiveness.

Historically, organizations have tended to be structured with all authority coming from a few individuals, or in some cases only a single individual. Examples of this are early family enterprises in which only the father and his children governed all phases of the business. Technical and management skills were of little importance in the early days before the industrial revolution because industries were small and lacked the competition of today's marketplace. The structure of this early organization was very simple: It was a huge subordinate group connected by a thin link to an extremely small management group on top. There was room in this system only for authority directed to subordinates through middle managers who enacted all decisions made from above. With little technical advancement going on in most markets, this system managed quite well up until the industrial revolution.

During this time of thriving technical achievement, businesses found it necessary to augment their organizational structure and improve upon their managerial strategies to keep pace with the emerging changes. No longer were organizations centrally staffed. Span of management, the number of individuals reporting directly to one superior, was contracted to better coordinate all functions of management. Organizations tended to decentralize power in contrast to prerevolutionary times. The newer structure of the organization began to take the shape of a pyramid. No longer could corporations sit idle and hope that the family, or central body, would dictate all directives no matter how minute. Authority began to be delegated downward, with improved rewards granted to all managers. This tended to develop energetic involved subordinates at lower levels of management.

As business complexity and technology advanced further, there became a need for even more specialists for each phase of management. A marketing manager, personnel supervisor, engineering director, and other specialists began to be represented in upper management. In today's dynamic technical society, management requirements have been met by a new formation or organizational structure. It resembles a large pyramid with a smaller pyramid balanced directly on top of it. Specialists are given higher authority positions ranging from advisors to direct supervision in the area of their expertise. Organizational structures will always have to be redefined and augmented to meet the ever-changing management requirements and marketing needs for the corporation's services or products. With this basic historical view of the organization, a more detailed discussion of the components and interactions of the organization may be pursued.

Unity of Command

The concept of *unity of command* was established by Henri Fayol.[1] He stated that "no member of an organization should report to more than one supervisor." This was and is today a very controversial idea. Followers of Fayol stated that confusion, loss of productivity, conflict, and poor morale were all symptoms of having subordinates answer to more than one supervisor. In actual practice this rule need not be absolutely rigid, prohibiting all but unified command. There are problems associated with unity of command in that subordinates must receive a flow of command or influence through only one supervisor. Since most managers usually lack expertise in every detailed aspect of their operation, specialists skills may be passed by for lack of availability, time, pride, or various other reasons. The solution of the unity of command problem lies in the proper utilization of staff personnel, possible use of the matrix organizational structure, and the informal organization to be discussed later in this chapter.

Division of Labor

The concept of assigning elements of a task to different workers is as old as human civilization. Cicero, for example, called it the very basis for civilization. In 1776, Adam Smith in his book *The Wealth of Nations* discussed the division of labor in detail by using examples of manufacturing.[2] He observed that several persons each manufacturing a steel pin produced considerably fewer pins during a work period than did the same number of persons working as specialists on assigned elemental tasks. The division of labor creates the need for coordination and therefore impacts organizational structure.

In a macro sense, there are two ways of classifying the division of labor. The first is by division or ranking of hierarchy of authority based on status within the company as shown in Figure 3.1. The second is to divide horizontally according to function as shown in Figure 3.2. In this form, the type of labor is the primary factor in determining how the work is divided. This is apparent if one considers, for example, the personnel, accounting, and engineering departments, which do not work together but must at some point be interconnected.

Examples of today's application of the Adam Smith division of labor concept would include the basic manufacturing process of most high-volume produced products, e.g., automobiles, appliances, and food. As a total manufacturing work task is more finely divided, the cycle time for each work station decreases, namely, more division of labor. Figure 3.3 depicts the general relationship between productive effort, namely, the percentage of labor expended that adds real value to a product, and the manufacturing cycle time. Cycle time is inversely proportional to the application of the division of labor concept. This same increase in productive effort as related to the division of labor also extends to professional level workers.

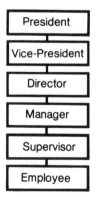

Figure 3.1   Vertical division of labor

Figure 3.2 Horizontal division of labor

The major benefit resulting from the division of labor is increased productivity. When efficiency is increased, output is increased, which means that operating costs are lower and profits higher.

Negative effects of division of labor are also present.[3] Output may increase, but product quality often will be lowered. This goes hand in hand with another problem—job dissatisfaction. Many people, both professional and direct hourly employees working on specialized jobs, have low job satisfaction that tends to lower concern for quality. A third negative effect, also related to the first two, is high personnel turnover. The hiring and training of new personnel is expensive, but the cost of replacing a person who leaves a subdivided job is less, since there is less to learn and as a result training costs are lower. The strategies to overcome the negative effects of division of labor as well as its specific effect on engineers and technicians are discussed in later chapters.

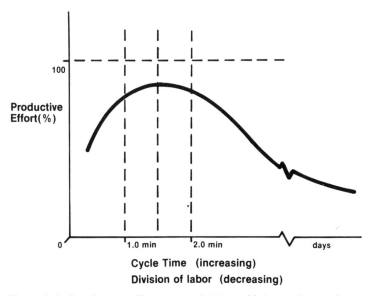

Figure 3.3 Productive effort versus division of labor and manufacturing cycle time

Line and Staff

Another way to divide jobs in an organization is by separating them into the *doers* and the *advisors*. Groups responsible for performing the main objectives of the organization are classified as *line*, and all others as *staff* or supportive personnel.

Staff groups perform three basic functions. First, they provide a service to the line organization by performing certain tasks which are needed but not absolutely necessary on a day-to-day basis for continuing operation of the organization, such as the design of new products. Second, staff gives advice on matters that fall within that group's area of knowledge, such as suitability of substituting new material. Third, staff acts as a control function. The staff tries to keep uniformity of policy administration in all organizational groups. In order to further clarify the rather complex nature of line-staff relationships, it is useful to look at a typical manufacturing firm. In this common type of organization, the *line management* usually is composed of those managers who direct units that are involved in the direct fabrication or assembly of the product. Line people are, in effect, those people who are involved with the major thrust of the business.

Staff people, on the other hand, are those individuals whose major responsibility is to serve the line and provide advice and service that is necessary or useful in producing or fabricating the product. Thus, in most manufacturing organizations, personnel, purchasing, industrial engineering, engineering, and financial units are staff. Because of their differing roles, engineers (staff) tend to focus on their speciality, and have a strong desire to excel in the application of both new ideas and technical knowledge. Line people tend to focus on shorter-term profits and those developments that are less risky or offer higher probabilities of success. Since line managers usually have the final authority with regard to product decisions, it is not unusual to find a bright young engineer who feels that his or her good ideas or developments are not being utilized effectively.

The above example reflects the differing set of needs, values, and expectations between these two groups. In fact, several factors lead to line-staff conflict. Staff personnel usually come from different backgrounds than line personnel. Persons working in staff positions are usually university trained and have a speciality. The second factor is a different set of task objectives and responsibilities. This is due to the fact that staff people strive to develop the most comprehensive solutions which are not always understandable by line personnel. Third, the two groups have different ways of gaining recognition. Staff personnel such as engineers are judged by the thoroughness of their plans, which will be seen by top executives, while the line people are concerned with high output and the workability of plans. Fourth, staff and line groups sometimes have different time goals. Staff is concerned with long-term results, but the line is most concerned with short-term output.

Historically, conflict between line and staff was intensified because of lines' resentment of staffs' superior education and tendency to assume line authority. In recent years the educational gap has narrowed substantially between these two groups, and the willingness of line managers to accept professional staff as an integral part of the organization has increased. Thus, the problem of line-staff conflict is not as great today as it was 20 years ago.

Since a sound and supportive line-staff relationship is important to engineering, scientific, and professional staff managers, several pointers are offered to improve this relationship:

1. Be sure line personnel are given credit for their accomplishments; remember that the staff role is basically advisory.

2. Do not usurp line authority. This kind of activity will cause line managers to become defensive, and impede the development of a constructive relationship. In fact, the end result will be less staff influence in the future.

3. Help line people solve their problems. This will pay large dividends in building future line-staff relationships.

4. Understand the nature and impact of interpersonal communication. The information on improving interpersonal communication skills contained in Chapter 7 will be useful in working with line personnel. Specifically, it is important for engineering, scientific, and professional staff managers to avoid communicating personal superiority when working with line employees.

5. Be cost conscious and assume a practical orientation concerning problems in which expertise is sought.

Span of Management

Span of management may be defined as the number of subordinates directly reporting to a manager. The term *span of management* is used instead of *span of control* because as Koontz and O'Donnell point out, "the span is one of management and not merely of control."[4] There is no exact rule for determining the correct span for any particular situation. In the 1930s V. A. Graicunas analyzed the problem of superior-subordinate relationships and developed the following mathematical expression:[5]

$$R = n \left[\frac{2^n}{2} + (n - 1) \right]$$

where

R = the number of all types of relationships that might concern management

n = the number of subordinates

The Graicunas expression considers not only the direct relationship between a superior and his or her immediate subordinates, but also the relationships with different groupings and the cross-relationships among subordinates. In practical application, very few managers engage in all relationships theoretically possible.

A more useful span of management expression can be developed to relate the total number of employees in the organization with the number of levels of management and the individual span of each manager. This expression is

$$N = \sum_{n=1}^{m} L_n(SC_n) + 1$$

where

N = the total number of personnel in the organizational structure

L_n = the number of managers at each organizational level

SC_n = the average number of subordinates reporting to each manager

Figure 3.4 depicts a flat organization with only two levels of management above the nonsupervisory personnel. Figure 3.5 shows a more vertical organization with four levels of management above the nonsupervisory personnel. Solving for the total number of personnel for the vertical organization (Figure 3.5) yields

$$N = \sum_{n=1}^{4} L_n(SC_n) + 1$$

$$= 16(4) + 4(4) + 2(2) + 1(2) + 1$$

$$= 87 \text{ employees}$$

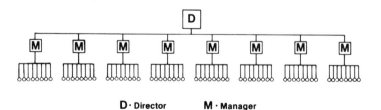

D· Director   M · Manager

Figure 3.4 Broad span of management with horizontal organization

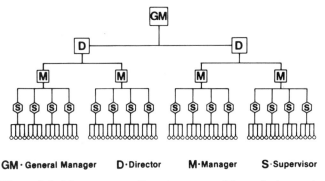

GM · General Manager   D · Director   M · Manager   S · Supervisor

Figure 3.5 Narrow span of management with vertical organization

This organization contains 64 nonsupervisory employees and 23 managers with spans ranging between 2 and 4. A similar calculation for the flat organization (Figure 3.4) yields 73 total personnel. The number of nonsupervisory employees totals 64, the same as the more vertical organization. Obviously, the difference is that the vertical organization contains 14 more managers.

An important aspect of this span of management relationship is that once any two of the three variables are determined, the third is set. For example, if we require a given number of nonsupervisory personnel and desire to limit the span of management, then the number of management levels is fixed along with the total number of employees in the organization.

In most organizations, the number of nonsupervisory personnel is determined by the enterprise operations. Consequently, the span of management decision is critical in determining the number of management levels and total organizational size. In a technically oriented department, a smaller span is normally more desirable. Where mass production and job specialization occurs, a manager can supervise a larger number of persons, especially if they perform similar tasks and their output is easily determined. In general, the acceptable span of control decreases with

Less predictable work demands.

Greater discretion allowed to the subordinates.

Greater job responsibility, as measured by the length of time between a decision and its review or results.

Greater task interdependence among subordinates. When subordinates work on simple, repetitive, and easily measured tasks, the span of control can be larger.

Table 3.1 Number of Executives Reporting to the President in 100 Large and
41 Medium-Sized Companies

No. of executives reporting to president	No. of large companies	No. of medium-sized companies
1	6	3
2	–	–
3	1	2
4	3	2
5	7	4
6	9	8
7	11	7
8	8	5
9	8	2
10	6	4
11	7	1
12	10	–
13	8	1
14	4	1
15	1	–
16	5	–
17	–	1
18	1	–
19	–	–
20	1	–
21	1	–
22	–	–
23	2	–
24	1	–
Totals	100	41

Source: Reprinted from Ernest Dale, *Planning and Developing the Company Organization Structure,* Research Report no. 20, American Management Association, New York, pp. 77-78.

As a guideline, four to seven subordinates is typical for engineering and technical problem-solving groups, while 20 to 25 or more may be managed at the first-level manufacturing supervisor position. Experience indicates that in most organizations the top manager has a span too làrge for the best operating effectiveness. Table 3.1 summarizes the results of a study to determine the number of executives reporting to the president in 100 large and 41 medium-sized companies. The average (arithmetic mean) number of executives reporting to the president was 9.64 in large companies and 7.00 in medium-sized companies.

Organizational Design

An organizational structure is the framework within which management and the operations of an organization are performed. The structure establishes formal authority as opposed to informal authority. This formal network of authority is the framework of who reports to whom and is usually documented on a diagram that shows the relative locations and reporting relationships of the units and management positions in the organization. If a sound organizational structure can be developed, it will improve the performance of the organization and also will make the people in the organization feel more comfortable, as their positions are clearly defined.

Organizational structure provides communication and coordination. By grouping jobs and people, the structure aids the communication between people working on the same job activities. An organizational structure determines the location of decision making within the organization. By varying the number of intermediary levels between the president or chief executive officer and each individual department in an organization, the locus of decision making is determined.

An organizational structure should create the proper balance and emphasis on activities. Activities considered important to a firm's success may be placed at higher levels in the organization in order to stress their importance. By being placed higher in the organization, there are less managers to interfere with and slow down communication, and the time required for decision making is greatly reduced. Activities of relatively equal ranking should be placed at similar management levels in the structure in order to insure that they will receive equal emphasis. This equalization will prevent one department's domination of another, a necessity for the firm's successful operation.

The following statement summarizes the design objectives for most organizational structures:

The organizational structure (1) must be logical and systematic and definitely fix responsibility and authority; (2) must be personal to the extent of taking into account the aspirations and needs of individual members; in this way the employee's good will is obtained; their best efforts are utilized and their business relations made pleasant; (3) must provide for cooperation between various divisions and levels of the undertaking; (4) be capable of modifications as may become necessary; and (5) facilitate decision making.[6]

Organizational Configurations

There are several standard organizational structures. Each of these have different characteristics that may fit the specific product and people needs of an organization. In actual practice, a firm's formal organization is usually a hybrid of two or more of the standard structures.

The functional structure has a pattern of departmentalization by major functions such as engineering, manufacturing, quality assurance, and marketing, as shown in Figure 3.6. This structure allows each manager to specialize in one area of activity, enabling them to gain knowledge and expertise in that particular area. In a functional organization, if someone develops a new process or idea, it is easily implemented in all areas since it was created for a particular problem solution possibly common to more than one product line. An example of an engineering department's organizational structure is also shown in Figure 3.6.

A limitation of functional organization is that one group may lose touch with another area. To prevent this it is necessary for a good network of communications to exist. Also, the coordination between groups may become difficult and

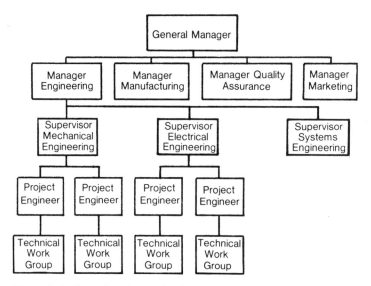

Figure 3.6 Functional organization

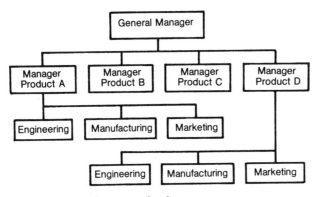

Figure 3.7   Product organization

conflicts may arise; therefore, a higher level manager may be required to alleviate differences among departments.

The product structure divides an organization by product line. This is depicted in Figure 3.7. The manager of each product is given the responsibility of all phases of operation from product design and manufacturing through all marketing functions. There are two general advantages of a product organization. The first is that the members have a tendency to feel they are in competition with other groups and may increase productive output to impress superiors and outperform other product lines. Secondly, a person is able to learn more as he or she is given a broader responsibility as compared to the relatively narrow knowledge requirements of the functional organization. This learning allows a manager to be more adaptable and qualified as promotional opportunities develop within the organization

The disadvantages of product organization can have serious effects on the profitability of the enterprise. An example of a major possible problem is that two different product lines may have the exact or at least a similar problem and both groups will assign engineers or other specialists to correct the problem. This is a waste of precious time and money due to the repetition of efforts.

A structure by territory as shown in Figure 3.8 divides the organization by regions or areas. This may be necessary if the product line varies or customer needs differ as the geography or other factors change. Also, an organization may have plants in different parts of the country, and operating conditions vary considerably from one area to another. In this type of situation, the area decentralization organization has advantages.

A client-oriented organizational structure is advantageous when each client is a large enough consumer to devote personnel and time to a specific interest

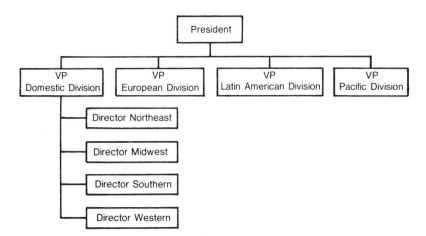

Figure 3.8 Organization by territory

group. An example of this type of organization (Figure 3.9) is one that does work for the general public and also the government or another mass buyer.

The last organization to be mentioned is the *matrix structure*. This structure involves departmentalization by function and by product. The dotted lines in Figure 3.10 represent a special organization clustered around product A and comprising personnel who are members of various functional departments. They are permanently assigned to engineering, manufacturing, quality assurance, and sales, but apply their effort to product A and work for the manager of product A. While the matrix organization violates the unity of command, the concept

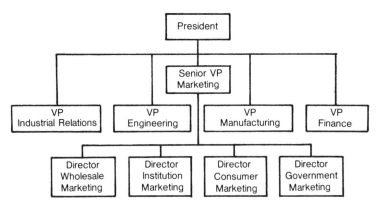

Figure 3.9 Organization by client

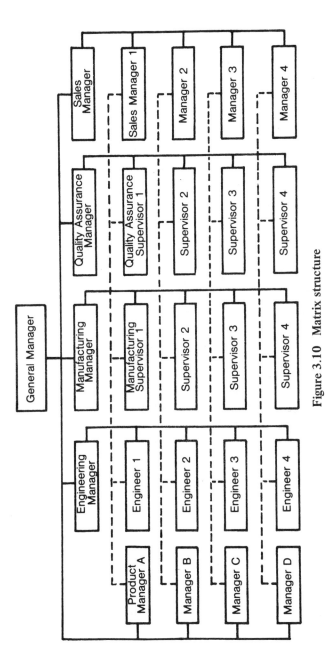

Figure 3.10 Matrix structure

will work if the product manager and the various functional managers interface well, especially as related to employee evaluation.

Selection of Personnel

It is both proper and functional for managers to select those new people who will work for them. Technical managers who work in organizations that have an effective personnel department can get useful aid in the selection process. Personnel departments often can provide help with preemployment screening which includes interviews, reference checks, and testing.

In recent years it has become necessary for managers to be more concerned with women and minorities among their applicants. Specifically, Title VII of the Civil Rights Act of 1964 as ammended by the Equal Employment Opportunity Act of 1972 clearly prohibits employment discrimination against any individual or group because of race, color, religion, or national origin. Several agencies of the federal government including the Equal Employment Opportunity Commission and the Office of Federal Contract Compliance are given the responsibility of enforcing the provisions of this legislation.

Technical managers who work for companies that do a large amount of business with the federal government should be particularly concerned with avoiding charges of discrimination in their hiring practices. Federal contracts may be witheld or canceled in cases where an investigating agency finds that discrimatory hiring practices are being used. It is important to note that the "result" of the hiring practices rather than "intent" is the real test. In other words, a manager may have no intention of discriminating in his or her hiring practices, but if these practices actually result in discrimination against women or minorities, the law is being violated. Again, personnel departments can provide a considerable amount of help and insight to technical managers in dealing with these kinds of hiring problems.

The major objective in the selection process is to get a good match between candidates and jobs. Managers should be concerned with a given candidate's skills and aptitudes, and his or her general level of personality and social development. While skills and aptitudes determine what can be accomplished on the job, personality and social factors often determine motivation or what will be accomplished. It is also important to consider the prospective employee's perception of future promotions and compensation increases, and determine if they are consistent with the company's plans. Thus, an accurate appraisal of these factors is necessary for good selection to take place.

The manager either independently or with the aid of the personnel department has available several tools that can help evaluate potential job candidates. The four most commonly used tools are the interview, application form, tests, and references. One study indicated that the interview was the most preferred and widely used selection tool.[7] According to this study managers prefer the interview because they believe that the interview is most effective in evaluating the "will do" job factors, namely, motivation, personality, and social development. There is a general consensus among a majority of managers that these latter factors are the most difficult to assess in the hiring process.

Technical managers should know that there are several weaknesses associated with the interview. For example, it may be biased, and decisions tend to be made early in the interview and are often based on incomplete information. Structured interviewing which uses predetermined questions conducted by two or more interviewers is a useful means of counteracting personal bias and increasing the accuracy of the appraisal. While for lower level jobs these additional interviews may be too costly and time consuming, for higher level positions the improved results may more than offset this additional cost.

Application forms and testing can also be useful in selection. However, in using each of these tools, the technical manager must be careful that they do not result in discrimination against women or minorities. For example, certain types of information regarding sex, race, and marital status can no longer be used legally in making hiring decisions unless such factors can be shown to a basic functional requirement of the position. Also, test results should be validated when used in hiring. Specifically, the employer should be able to show a correlation between test scores and job performance. Finally, references can be of some help in establishing character and previous employment record.

An accurate, up-to-date job description is extremely useful when selecting candidates for a given job. This description should include an identification of the duties of the job, performance requirements, and the general level of difficulty associated with performing the assigned duties. An accurate description of this latter group of factors is very helpful in attaining a good match between the personality and social makeup of the candidate and the intrinsic content of the job. It is usually wise to solicit input from current incumbents in developing accurate job descriptions which include stating performance requirements for these positions. In addition to improving the quality of selection, performance requirements or standards are an effective basis for evaluating the new employee on the job (see Chapter 11).

Any special managerial attention given to the hiring process will pay large dividends. Absenteeism, turnover, and motivation problems are costly to both the managers in time and effort, and to the firm in "bottom line" results. A good selection program reduces absenteeism, turnover, and can substantially improve employee performance; consequently, the proper selection of new employees is an important managerial function. While a thorough understanding of the second half of this book which deals with the behavioral aspects of management is crucial in improving selection skills, a knowledge of the material contained in Chapter 6 on individual and group needs is particularly beneficial.

38

Summary

In choosing a structure the manager has to select the one that best meets the requirements for the total organization. There are several factors to consider in making this decision. These include environment, tasks and technology, and people and coordination requirements.

Two important variables in an organization's environment are its stability and diversity. Some companies may face a relatively stable, predictable demand for their products or services, while others face rapid and unpredictable changes. Examples of areas that must be monitored for stability include labor markets, reliability of suppliers, technology, and political and economic conditions. These are all areas that the organization and manager must adapt to if the firm is going to be successful.

Functional organizational structures provide the greatest institutional commitment to permanence. They help the firm establish routines and patterns suited to predictable environments. A major disadvantage is that because they are more suited to stable environments, they often hamper a firm's ability to cope with instability in the outside environment.

Product, territory, and client-oriented organizations are by definition more flexible. They allow the addition or subtraction of a structure unit as conditions change. Structural flexibility inside the organization helps cope with instability outside of the organization.

The coordination between various groups must be watched when choosing a structure and designing its component parts. Cooperation must exist between different departments; if there is little cooperation or coordination, the organization will suffer. An example would be the need for coordination between sales and product development. Because of their field contact the personnel in sales are more likely to have the most knowledge of customer needs and wants. A high level of cooperation will allow product development to meet customer demands without wasting time on low priority activities.

The educational level of the employees in an organization is a clue to choosing the best structural type. People of modest education may often be hired to fill jobs that have well-established routines, while those of higher talent most often are hired to fill jobs where competence and flexibility are required. In organizational design, one must be careful to maintain organizational structure in relation to the educational levels of available personnel. As more individuals obtain higher educations, rigid structures often "cramp their style." A flexible structure like the product-oriented type will easily allow the addition or deletion of units. The type of structure that an organization chooses will have a great effect on its productivity. An examination of the company's environment, the tasks within the operation, and the characteristics of the personnel are of paramount importance in choosing a structure. The choice must be made with one central consideration in mind: *Given the firm's goals and strategy, which structure will help it cope most effectively with its environment?* This question should be kept in the executive's mind when it is time to make or change an organizational structure.

The structure can be defined graphically with a formal outline of the organization. This outline indicates the names of departments and individuals with job titles and the relationships among all units. In addition to the graphical outline, an organizational manual is useful. The manual should indicate the duties and responsibilities of each job. It has been stated that this manual is the final documentation of the organizational design process. It clearly delineates the objectives of each organizational unit, the scope of authority of the manager of each unit, and its relationship to other units. If relationships to organizations outside the company are part of a particular job, these relationships are also defined. The organizational manual is also very useful for orienting new personnel to their jobs.[8]

This chapter highlights the problem and importance of good employee selection. It is clear that many useful tools are available to improve the match of individuals and jobs. Technical managers can improve their unit's performance by understanding the nature of these tools which includes their strengths, weaknesses, and applicability.

Notes

1. H. J. Fayol, *General and Industrial Administration,* Sir Isaac Pitman and Sons, London, 1949.

2. Adam Smith, *The Wealth of Nations,* Clarendon Press, Oxford, 1976.

3. R. Boyer and R. L. Shell, End of the Line at Lordstown. *Business and Society Review,* no. 3, Autumn 1972, pp. 31-35.

4. H. Koontz and C. O'Donnell, *Principles of Management,* 4th ed., McGraw-Hill, New York, 1968, p. 241.

5. V. A. Graicunas, Relationship in Organization, reprinted in L. Gulick and L. Urwick (eds.), *Papers on the Science of Administration,* Institute of Public Administration, New York, 1937, pp. 181-187.

6. John A. Logan, Harry Rubey, and Walker W. Milner, *The Engineer and Professional Management,* 3rd ed., Iowa State University Press, Aimes, Iowa, 1970.

7. D. D. Martin, W. J. Kearney, and G. D. Holdefer, The Decision to Hire: A Comparison of Selection Tools. *Business Perspectives,* vol. 7, no. 3, Spring 1971, pp. 11-15.

8. Kenneth Case, Joe H. Mize, and Wayne C. Turner, *Introduction to Industrial and Systems Engineering,* Prentice-Hall, Englewood Cliffs, N.J., 1978.

4

Directing and Controlling

Introduction

Direction and controlling are two essential aspects of management. Early approaches considered planning, organizing, and controlling the three fundamental parts of management, but through the influence of the behaviorists, directing is now considered equally important. Controlling is concerned with the regulation of business activities in relation to the original plan. Directing can be defined as the guiding of work toward the accomplishment of organizational objectives. The importance and use of directing and controlling for technical managers can be shown by examining the following: responsibility, authority, delegation, salary administration, feedback, work measurement, performance appraisal, budgeting, information systems, and critical path scheduling.

Responsibility

Responsibility is considered to be the foundation of control and direction. It may be defined as the obligation to execute functions or work.

The division of responsibility must be decided upon so that a company can operate properly. First the work must be divided among available personnel. Hopefully, a person with the right skills and abilities can be found for each job. Once this is done, jobs with similar objectives and requirements are grouped together to form a section. A manager with the right qualifications is then selected to supervise the section of workers. In this simple arrangement the supervisor is responsible for the output of the entire group. The guide to this kind of grouping is called *functional similarity*. This is simply the process of putting like functions together. Functional similarity usually leads to specialization.

The concept of functional similarity is basic to the process of dividing responsibility and delegating authority. However, functional similarity cannot always be used. For example, quality control is similar to many manufacturing operations, yet it must be kept separate to insure that it will not be biased. Often it may be advantageous to create internal competition and keep similar operations separate. In a small organization it is not uncommon to have two dissimilar operations in the same group. Typical examples are the grouping of product design and prototype building and testing, shipping and receiving, and the grouping of computer operations and finance.

There are three other important guidelines to follow in dividing and delegating responsibility: Avoid gaps, overlaps, and delegation of responsibility for work that is not part of the objective. Overlap is when two or more people are responsible for the same function. This is usually caused by unclear boundaries or vague directions and orders from higher level management. Large firms usually have overlap problems when duplicate work is done in different parts of the organization. Overlap creates controversy and sometimes leads to groups fighting about the overlap area. When this occurs the overlap area is usually desired by both groups to enhance their power. More often than not, when the work is extremely difficult or where the effort may go unnoticed by higher management, the overlap area will be neglected by both parties. A gap is the failure to foresee all requirements for the effective accomplishment of goals. A gap is usually created when an area is unforeseen in the original plan or any updated plan. The dangers of this are that the function may never get done, and if it is done it may be attempted by someone not qualified for the job.

Authority

As stated earlier, authority is derived from responsibility. Authority can be defined as the power to decide, to command, and to perform. It can also be defined as formal power to act or power freely granted. Authority has been traditionally thought of as being obtained from the high levels of management and passed on to lower levels. However, with the development of the informal authority idea and acceptance theory, the traditional view must be modified.

Informal authority is the authority an organization does not plan. It exists in the lower levels of the organization and generates upward instead of downward. It may or may not follow the formal structure of the organization.

An important idea concerning authority is the Barnard-Simon theory, often referred to as *acceptance theory*.[1] This theory states that authority exists only when subordinates accept the commands as authoritative. The theory is also consistent with the traditional idea of authority by reasoning that when individuals accept authority from above, they do so because they recognize the support of top management. The value of this theory is that it recognizes the individual's decision to accept authority as the key to the existence of authority. In order to get the individual to accept authority it may be necessary to use positive rewards

42

or negative sanctions. The theory also emphasizes the importance of leadership qualities. The leadership style of a manager can determine how much of his or her authority will be accepted by subordinates. Thus, the Barnard-Simon theory shifts the emphasis from the traditional thought of authority existing merely because it comes from above to the theory where the support and acceptance of authority by subordinates determines its existence. There are six basic types of authority:

Authority from outside

Authority from position

Authority from personal attributes

Line authority

Staff authority

Functional authority

Although authority rests in a position, its source may be external to the organization to which it belongs. For example, a law enforcement person is given certain authority by laws passed by the city council. The council in turn is elected by the people, who are defined as the ultimate source for all authority. If a person does not feel that "the people" are the ultimate source of authority, he or she will not accept this source and will probably act differently from those who do.

Authority from position is based on the notion that in most organizations and social situations certain individuals become recognized for being skilled, capable, and competent. Their advice is sought and their instructions are accepted, provided that the complying person believes that the expertise is being used to his or her advantage.

Authority from personal attributes is authority that resides in a person and comes from what is often called charisma, which may be projected by appearance and behavior.

Line authority is the formal power to act over and command all operations and functions within a particular part of the organization. An example of this is an assembly supervisor who has control over certain parts of the production line, or a chief draftsman in charge of completing final engineering drawings. Staff authority is the ability to advise line management on the performance of line functions.

Staff authority carries no power to give orders directly or make decisions. It usually exists in special areas and should only be used to advise or consult with line managers. An example would be an industrial engineer assigned to study the problems of a manufacturing process. When the study is completed the engineer has no power to alter the process; he or she can only present the findings to the line manager for a decision. Another example would be the product designer recommending a specific vendor for material procurement.

The power to command within a certain area of expertise is called *functional authority*. Examples of these areas include maintenance, law, medical, accounting, and computer systems.

Authority is one of two sources of power; the other is force. The threat of force alone is usually enough to make most people yield. People are seldom fired for displeasing the boss; the fear of being humiliated or considered incompetent is perhaps the most common threat for technical managers.

The power of authority can be divided into three categories: office, knowledge, and character. As previously discussed, the authority of office is the power given to someone simply because he or she is the boss. The authority of knowledge is the power delegated because one is an expert in a particular field. Managers may be given this power even though they are less able to perform certain detail tasks as well as subordinates. An example would be the manager of a research laboratory. The manager may know less about a test procedure than a lower level technician, yet it is the overall knowledge of that specific experiment and all the other experiments being conducted that gives the manager the power of authority. Perhaps the most important power is authority of character. This power has to be earned. Its major components are honesty of purpose, truthfulness, openness, good will, and good manners. Charm in this case is unimportant. It may be stated that "no one trusts a smoothy." Reliance on the authority of character as the chief ingredient in managerial leadership excludes the use of force and the generation of fear. Fear may be the worst enemy of managerial productivity.

Delegation

Delegation is the distribution of responsibility and authority within an organization. Stated another way, delegation is the decentralization of decision making.

Authority is delegated from a manager to a subordinate. The superior creates a relationship based on obligation between the superior and the subordinate; although the superior delegates authority, he or she is not relieved of the responsibility. It must be remembered that delegation only allows for someone else to do the work.

Whenever a manager delegates authority, a risk is created. The risk is that the subordinate may fail, leaving not only the subordinate to take the blame, but also the person who delegated the authority. Some managers attempt to avoid risk by limiting delegation and retaining all responsibility. Usually this is a poor policy because even in the smallest organization one manager cannot handle the total work load volume. Delegation also becomes necessary when the work load of a management position exceeds the physical and psychological capacity of one person. While delegation reduces the manager's work load in one respect, it adds to the work load by increasing the span of management.

Another argument for greater decentralization is the need to develop initiative and self-reliance among subordinates. Many executives believe that subordinates should be constantly challenged. The personality of the executive may also effect the extent of delegation. The psychological makeup of some executives inhibits their willingness to delegate decision-making prerogatives. A refusal to delegate may also be promoted by the degree of risk involved. Hard times and increased business competition for the organization may foster centralization. The organization's ability to absorb a mistake by a subordinate may be greatly reduced under these circumstances.

Technical managers are often reluctant to release authority. One reason for refusing to delegate authority is that there is no one in the organization qualified to handle it. Another reason is that many managers enhance their indispensibility to the enterprise by retaining authority. The most undesirable reason for not delegating authority is that a manager may not have sufficient delegating skills.

The ability and willingness to delegate authority to others is the essence of being a manager. Not to delegate should be considered a management failure.

Salary Administration and Incentives

Many technical managers are concerned with the salary administration of non-exempt (hourly paid) workers. The basic wage system for manual jobs encompasses four dimensions: (1) Pay related to effort; (2) the size of the unit for which rewards are calculated; (3) the proportion of total take-home pay, which is variable; and (4) the way in which payment can be linked to an assortment of performance indicators such as output, quality, and cost. In salary administration in most situations, the pay system should be a combination of these dimensions.

These dimensions must be considered in the context of two important variables, namely, internal and external consistency. *Internal consistency* refers to the level of pay associated with the various jobs within the organization. Pay rates are considered to be internally consistent when those jobs in the organization with greater perceived value pay higher rates than jobs of lesser perceived value. Lack of internal consistency leads to wage inequities which upset the employee motivation process and complicate managerial problems.

There are several tools that are widely used in helping a manager attain internally consistent relationships among wage rates. Since the application of these plans is usually quite involved, the technical manager should seek outside help in using them. In larger or smaller firms with a good personnel department, the personnel director is an appropriate and useful source of advice and help to the technical manager. Sometimes it takes several months or even years to correct widespread internal wage inequities. Since employees are very resistant to any managerial action that lowers their wage rates, many of these problems are corrected through employee transfer and attrition.

External consistency refers to the comparison of wages paid within the organization to wage rates paid outside the organization for similar jobs. When these rates are comparable to each other, a given firm's wage rates are considered to be externally consistent. External consistency is a desirable condition because it enables the manager to attract quality workers and reduces turnover among more capable employees. Good personnel departments usually have wage survey data available that indicate when wage rates need adjusting to meet the competitive market.

Payment by results is not always the best pay system, because a poorly developed set of standards and controls can upset internal consistency, which results in perceived wage inequities among employees and increased stress on management. A number of studies involving workers in manufacturing have indicated that lower output may result from this type of wage payment. Workers sometimes develop the habit of performing at slower rates for each job so that output standards are not changed. Another alternative is to record a lower production output and then apply the surplus time to a more difficult task. Most workers make little effort to reach bonus levels on difficult jobs. A result of this situation is that many workers have surplus time which is spent not working at all. Consequently, work standards are distorted and production is generally less efficient. The solution to this problem lies in the establishment of correct and fair output standards with proper employee incentives.

Allowances for waiting, process, and development activities can be used to obtain a more consistent salary administration program. Waiting allowances are used where frequent delays occur due to material shortages, breakdowns, or other problems. Process allowances can be paid to workers who only control their own rate of working for a portion of the time, the rest being machine-paced. Development allowances can be paid to workers whose jobs are being modified or have just been introduced.

Some salary administration plans provide a fixed bonus rate. Under the system bonus pay is fixed and is related to an agreed level of work output. The manager must accept the responsibility for ensuring that workers will achieve output targets. The manager should also encourage workers to contract for higher levels of output and pay.

When a successful incentive program exists, there also exists harmony between workers and management. One of the requirements for successful incentives is that the pay/effort/output relationship is clearly understood by all concerned personnel, both workers and management.[2]

When a company's incentive system is failing, it leads to poor management-worker relationships and causes morale problems. A common cause of failure is

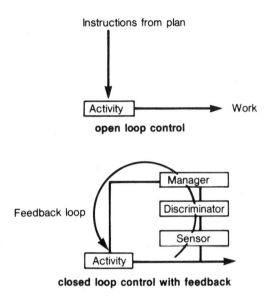

Figure 4.1   The control process

that the rewards are too remote or ill-defined for an individual to increase his or her work commitment.[3]

Control Systems

The control process can be represented by either open loop or closed loop forms as shown in Figure 4.1. An open loop control system is one that either needs no further control or cannot be further controlled once it is activated. The system is guided by a predetermined set of fixed instructions or laws that are not affected by any comparison between actual and planned conditions. Once the system is activated it will run its course regardless of what is happening. A dishwasher is a physical example of an open loop system. The dishwasher does not decide to turn on just because the dishes are dirty; it must be told what to do. The washing is done over a predetermined time, so it stops whether the dishes are clean or not. Open loop control conditions are also found in technical management situations. An undesirable example would be an engineering manager continuing the development of a new product without any reference or regard to the pre-planned budget.

The closed loop control system provides for both the comparison of actual conditions to a predetermined standard and the ability to make corrective action when deemed necessary. Attached to the system being controlled is a feedback loop. A simple physical example of feedback control is a thermostat controlling the temperature of a building. The element of control begins when the temperature of the building drops below a desired temperature, say 65°F. The furnace turns on until this desired temperature is reached and then turns off. There is a sensing device located in the thermostat that measures the temperature and sends impulses to the furnace whenever more heat is required. While the furnace is operating, the sensing device is constantly checking the temperature until the predetermined temperature is reached. Control with feedback is obviously desired in most management situations.

In a pure, ideal system, open loop control provides no feedback mechanism or corrective action and closed loop control implies continuous monitoring and correction. In actual practice all management systems eventually have a feedback loop, even though a system may appear to be an open loop process. Using the previously cited example of the product engineering manager, how long could one proceed without any reference or regard to a preplanned budget?

Feedback is the heart of any major control system where information is reported. The principal objective of feedback is to identify the sources of undesirable performance and make corrections.

Performance Measurement

Performance measurement is information about the system variables that the manager chooses to monitor and control. The system under the direction of a technical manager usually consists of many subsystems.[4] The system and subsystems almost always have multiple objectives. Each objective is usually influenced by several variables within the organization. Consequently, multiple measures of performance are required for effective control. While a person's motivation is an extraordinarily important factor in his or her subsequent performance, it is not the only factor. The employee must also have the ability to do what he or she has the motivation to do.[5] Performance depends on the ability possessed. For example, motivation in Air Force students was varied experimentally by telling one group that their performance in a complex task would be an important factor in their future assignment (conditions of high motivation) and giving another group of the same size the same task but without the information (conditions of no explicit motivation). As expected, the group operating under the conditions of high motivation had a higher level of performance than the other group. Each group had within it students who had demonstrated high ability in previous exercises and others who had demonstrated low ability. In comparing the groups, the high ability students increased their performance significantly more than the low ability students under the same conditions of high motivation. This suggests that the relationship between ability and motivation is multiplicative and can be expressed as follows:

$$Performance = f[(ability)(motivation)]$$

One first interpretation of this equation would be that ideally the relationship between performance and motivation is linear. However, there seems to be evidence that the relationship is curvilinear and would take the shape of an inverted parabola.

Budgets

Prior to the beginning of any major project or planning activity, a budget should be constructed. In addition to its value in the control process, a budget is frequently used to communicate plans to various parts of the organization. Budgets should be related logically and quantitatively to the business activities necessary to achieve planning objectives. Some organizations have budgetary systems encompassing each phase of planning and control of operations, while other organizations have partial budget systems concerned with particular aspects of the planning problem.

There are many types of budgets. The long-range and operations planning budget forecasts relationships between revenues and cost. The budgeting process

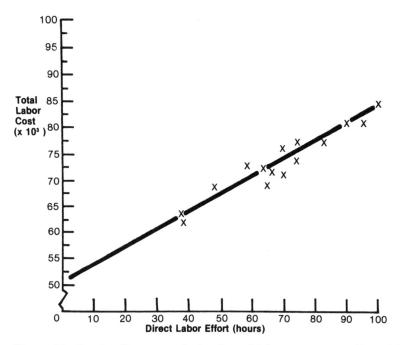

Figure 4.2 Scatter diagram analysis of total labor cost versus direct labor hours

usually starts with the preparation of a sales forecast which, after approval, makes it possible to prepare sales, marketing, engineering, production, and other necessary budgets. For example, the materials budget lists the types and amounts of raw materials, parts, and supplies required for the production of the finished product listed in the production budget. There should also be budgets that detail the cost of operating departments and labor budgets that detail the cost of labor for production of the finished product.[6]

The life or time cycle of a budget is influenced by such factors as the time necessary to complete merchandise turnover, the duration of the production cycle, the timing of purchase operations, and the pattern of seasonal variations. Some organizations budget ahead for a period of a year, with quarterly and monthly breakdowns at the time the budget is prepared. Quarterly revisions should be made in the budgets if the original forecasts and estimates are not in accord with the actual course of events. Monthly revisions are made occasionally due to forecasting and/or planning difficulties. An annual, semiannual, and quarterly budget may be maintained by adding another month after each monthly revision of budget estimates. Some special purpose and project budgets have a life span of only a few weeks or months.

The flexible budgeting concept is also useful in cost control. It can be used to set expense allowances for stated levels of output. If properly established the budget can also predict what costs should be at an achieved level of output. When output fluctuates, a flexible budget can predict how cost will change.

Many times a study of expenses can be made by constructing a simple scatter diagram of dollars spent versus actual output. A number of curve-fitting techniques can be used to fit the best curve through the data points (see Chapter 2). For example, if direct labor hours are plotted versus labor dollars expended, the resulting graph represents indirect labor costs, as shown in Figure 4.2.

This control procedure requires an explanation of any significant variance in the data. The budget can be separated into expense items controllable by the manager and those that are not under his or her control. Correction is usually directed toward the controllable items.

The budget should be continually examined, and any variations should be explainable.

Management Information Systems

The direction and control of an organization is enhanced by a management information system (MIS). The MIS may be defined as an automated system which presents information, both internal and external to the business, that aids in making a specific set of routine decisions. Two aspects of this definition should be clarified. First, the purpose of the MIS is to aid decision making and not to automate the decision-making process itself. As a result, the decision maker should have the dominant role, not the MIS. This means that any attempt to design a system without the support of management is pointless. The second aspect is that the MIS should focus on routine decisions only.

Experience has uncovered several incorrect assumptions which help account for the failure of countless MIS projects. The first is that managers commonly suffer from a lack of relevant information. Although there is some truth to this, it seems more realistic to say that they suffer more from too much irrelevant information. Therefore, the MIS should do away with this type of information rather than just focusing on supplying relevant information. The second assumption is that MIS systems should be based on the kinds of information that managers need. Since many managers do not understand the structure displayed in some decision or control situations, they will likely ask for more information than is needed. This way they play it safe. The point is that any analysis should start with the decision or control process, and the MIS should be a subsystem of that process. Thirdly, if a manager has all the information needed, the decision or control function will improve. This can be proved incorrect by a simple example. Consider a traveling salesman who has calls to make in 25 different cities. The best (least travel time) path should be determined. If the driving time between each pair of cities is known, it is unlikely that a manager could quickly decide the best travel path. A more appropriate approach would be to either provide the traveler with a decision rule or by using a model, compute the travel path with minimum travel time. This example shows that whenever information is given to a manager, it is necessary to consider how the data should be used. The last erroneous assumption is that a manager does not have to understand how the information system works to use it. If the person making decisions or active in the control process does not understand how the information system works, he or she will probably lack confidence in the system and it will therefore be of little real value to them.

There are a few fundamental MIS considerations necessary for effective control. The first is to identify the vital information for the organization. Another consideration is how often the system should be reviewed and modified. Finally, the MIS system should be cost effective.

The success of an information system depends on the availability of competent MIS managers and technicians who are well informed in the organization's policies, and the appropriate computer technology to support the total system.[7]

Critical Path Scheduling

A major part of controlling and directing a project is the scheduling of the *critical path*. The critical path is defined as the most time-consuming series of tasks in a project from start to completion. Figure 4.3, for example, depicts three paths for the project. The program evaluation and review technique (PERT) is a useful scheduling tool to assist in project control. It provides management with the ability to plan the best possible use of resources and to achieve a given goal

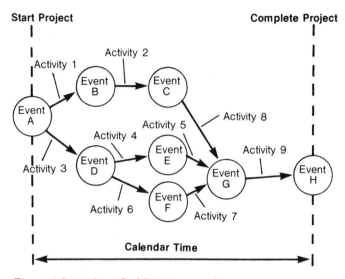

Figure 4.3   A simplified PERT network

within overall time and cost limitations. PERT enables managers to control unique programs, and handle the uncertainties involved in programs where little standard time data are available.

The development of PERT came about when programs arose that could not be managed with simple Gantt activity/time bar charting. It was first used by the Navy in 1958 and is now used on most national defense development programs. Additionally, PERT is used in the construction industry, in large manufacturing programs, and in developmental engineering projects.

Three basic requirements have been established for the use of PERT. The first requirement is that necessary tasks must be visualized in a clear enough manner to be included in a network comprised of events and activities as depicted in Figure 4.3. An event is defined as a specific accomplishment at a particular instant in time. An activity is defined as the time and/or resources necessary to progress from one event to the next. For example Activity 1 represents the work and time to progress from event A (start of project) to event B. This network requires sufficient precision so that there is no difficulty in monitoring actual accomplishment as the program proceeds.

The second requirement is that events and activities must be sequential in the network under a logical set of ground rules which allow the determination of critical and subcritical paths. One of the ground rules is that no successor event can be considered complete until all of the predecessor events have been completed. Another ground rule is that no looping can take place. An example would be that no successor event can have an activity dependence which leads back to a predecessor event.

The third requirement makes use of three time estimates for activities: optimistic, most likely, and pessimistic. The optimistic estimate assumes the minimum time an activity will take if all project activities are completed without difficulty. The most likely estimate assumes normal or average difficulties and represents the time that would be required if the activity could be repeated several times. The pessimistic estimate assumes the maximum time an activity should require given some initial project failure and above average difficulty.

The PERT time estimate for an activity conforms to the beta distribution as shown in Figure 4.4. Consequently, the mean time can be calculated using the following equation:

$$T_e = \frac{(t_o + 4t_m + t_p)}{6}$$

where

T_e = mean of beta distribution = the mean estimate for an activity

t_o = optimistic time estimate

t_m = most likely time estimate

t_p = pessimistic time estimate

and for the standard deviation,

$$\sigma = \left(\frac{t_p - t_o}{6}\right)^2$$

The use of PERT requires constant updating for effective project control. In most projects at least a biweekly reevaluation is useful. Sometimes valid means of shortening lead times along the critical path must be determined by applying new resources or additional funds. It is also necessary on occasion to change the scope of the work on the critical path to meet a required schedule.

There are many benefits gained by the use of PERT. The network development forces thinking about all project components, and the critical path analysis

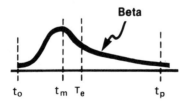

Figure 4.4   Distribution of PERT time estimates

may reveal problems not obvious by conventional planning methods. In addition, the PERT time estimating methodology tends to improve accuracy. Perhaps the most important benefit of PERT is that it allows a large amount of planning data to be presented in a format ideal for project control.

The path times for a PERT network may be estimated by calculating times for each activity and summing for a given path. Using the network shown in Figure 4.3 to illustrate, assume that time estimates and their standard deviations are as follows:

Activity	Time estimate (T_e)	Standard deviation (σ)
1	6.0	1.2
2	8.5	1.4
3	2.0	0.1
4	10.0	1.6
5	7.5	2.1
6	4.3	0.9
7	12.1	2.7
8	1.4	1.0
9	3.6	0.8

Path times are summed as follows:

Path	Time estimates (ΣT_e)		Total time
ABCGH	6.0 + 8.5 + 1.4 + 3.6	=	19.5
ADEGH	2.0 + 10.0 + 7.5 + 3.6	=	23.1
ADFGH	2.0 + 4.3 + 12.1 + 3.6	=	22.0

For this network the critical path ADEGH has a total time of 23.1 and total standard deviation of 4.6 (obtained by summing 0.1 + 1.6 + 2.1 + 0.8). From basic statistics, one standard deviation implies there is a 68 percent probability that the actual time required for the project will be 23.1 ± 4.6 or lie between 18.5 and 27.7 time units. There would be a 95 percent probability (plus or minus 2σ) of completing the project in 23.1 ± 9.2 or between 13.9 and 32.3 time units.

Summary

Directing and controlling are two essential aspects of management that impact on the functions of responsibility, authority, and delegation. Responsibility is the obligation to execute functions or work that is divided among available personnel. Authority is the power to decide, to command, and to perform. The traditional origin of authority implies that it is obtained from high levels of management within the formal organization and transmitted on to lower levels. Today, informal authority also exists within the organization and generates upward instead of downward. It may or may not follow the formal structure of the organization. Acceptance theory states that authority exists only when subordinates accept commands as authoritative, thus recognizing the importance of individual perception regarding power within the organization. The power of authority can be derived from office (formal boss), knowledge (the expert) and character (earned respect). Delegation is the distribution of responsibility and authority within an organization, or the decentralization of decision making. Management effectiveness requires that authority be delegated from superior to subordinate. Not to delegate should be considered a management failure.

A number of other management concerns have been discussed in this chapter. The importance of proper salary administration and incentives and performance measurement to the success of the technical organization was considered. The concepts of open loop and closed loop control as applied to management were discussed. The budget process and a supportive computer based management information system are requisites for proper direction and control. Critical path scheduling is an important methodology to define the most time-consuming series of tasks in a project from start to completion. The program evaluation and review technique (PERT) is a widely utilized and proven critical path scheduling and follow-up technique.

Notes

1. W. Warren Haynes and Joseph L. Massie, *Management: Analysis, Concepts, and Cases,* 2nd ed., Prentice-Hall, N.J., 1969, pp. 161-162.

2. R. L. Shell and D. S. Shupe, *Wage Incentives for Solid Waste Collection Personnel,* Environmental Protection Technology Series, EPA-600/2-77-019, U.S. Environmental Protection Agency, 1977.

3. R. L. Shell and D. S. Shupe, Productivity: Hope for City Woes. *Industrial Engineering,* vol. 8, no. 12, December 1976.

4. R. L. Shell and E. M. Malstrom, "Measurement and Enhancement of Work-force Productivity in Service Organizations," *Proceedings, Twenty-Fifth Annual Joint Engineering Management Conference,* 1977.

5. D. F. Byers and R. L. Shell, "Evaluation of Work Activity in a Technical Library," *Proceedings, Seventh Annual Conference, American Society for Information Systems,* 1978.

6. J. Paperman and R. L. Shell, The Accounting Approach for Performance Measurement. *Journal of Purchasing and Materials Management,* Summer 1977.

7. R. L. Shell, "Data Processing/Computers and Future Technology," *Proceedings, Tenth Annual Conference, American Technical Education Association,* October 1976.

5
Decision Making

The Decision-making Process

A decision is the selection of the preferred course of action from two or more alternatives. The decision-making process may be the result of hunch or "gut feelings," or may be based on a scientific approach. This approach considers a clear understanding of goals, comparative alternatives, and consistent priorities.

The decision-making environment has two extremes: decision making under known conditions, and decision making under uncertain conditions. The amount of risk associated with the decision depends on the amount of uncertainty, namely, risk increases with uncertainty. Many decisions are made with inherent conflict concerning goals. For example, marketing would like extensive product features and diversity to enhance sales, while manufacturing desires product standardization to minimize production costs. Another example of goal conflict would be team marketing and manufacturing, both wanting large inventories to provide rapid response to customer needs with minimum production delays, against the financial goals of the organization. A major concern of top management is to make decisions that resolve these types of conflicts and realize the best outcome for overall corporate objectives.

Some decisions are simple, while others are more complex. Simon classified decisions as *programmed* and *nonprogrammed*.[1] Programmed decisions are those associated with routine and well-structured problems. Examples include decisions for production scheduling, payroll, and product pricing. Nonprogrammed decisions are associated with nonroutine and poorly structured problems. Examples include facility design considerations, new product development, and policy establishment. Most programmed decisions can be computerized for essentially automatic handling. Nonprogrammed decisions may only be partially solved or assisted with computerization.

56

Many decisions require an acceptable solution to a problem. As with the selection of the "best" alternative, there is usually more than one "best" solution
to any given problem. The initial approach to problem solving is usually undertaken within the framework of one's own experience. Other approaches include
the experience of others, analytical techniques, or a combination of two or more
of these approaches. In any case, it is useful to remember that creativity is important in many decisions. One should not attempt to reinvent the wheel when a
standard wheel will suffice, but a large percentage of nonprogrammed decisions
can be improved with creative input from management. The input may be based
on experience or science, or just serendipity (recognizing valuable things not
specifically sought).

An important point concerning the decision-making process is that judgment
appears to improve with experience. While most researchers and practicing managers agree with this, it should be remembered that innate ability is also required.
Good managers should profit from their mistakes and from their successes.

Systems Analysis Aids Decision Making

The systems analysis approach structures a methodology for decision making
that analyzes problems to find the most effective and efficient solution within
certain constraints. The approach discussed in the sections that follow is taken
from Shell and Stelzer.[2]

Basic Steps of Systems Analysis

The systems analysis methodology for decision making is composed of the following basic steps:

Define the problem

Define the objectives

Define the alternatives

Make assumptions concerning the system

Define the constraints

Define the criteria

Collect the data

Build the model

Evaluate the alternatives

Defining the problem may appear to be a needless step since this is the basic
reason the analysis is being undertaken, but it is probably the most important

step in the procedure. In the definition of the problem there must be an accurate description of the present situation showing some sort of disparity that must be eliminated. The process of determining exactly "what is wrong" can be the most consuming part of the entire analysis and the most critical, for the most perfect solution to the wrong problem does nothing to solve the real problem.

Objectives must be defined to provide a structural framework and overall goals for the systems analysis. Clearly stated objectives are also useful for establishing limits and guidelines for the remaining basic steps.

The definition of alternatives should be exhaustive, even though some alternatives are obviously inferior. The reasoning behind this is that some new constraints might arise, making the superior alternatives impossible to implement. These alternatives represent the competing "systems" for accomplishing the objectives. They present opposing strategies, policies, or specific actions, including the required fiscal and physical resources.

Assumptions must be made about the larger system within which the alternatives will work. This system should include anything that affects the problem situation or the alternatives. Of course, facts are much more desirable than assumptions, but it is not always possible to know or predict precisely how things will be in the future. The statistical sensitivity of these assumptions will have to be tested when the model is built. This can be accomplished by modifying different assumptions and observing the effect on the desired output.

It is difficult to identify all constraints. However, more information about problem restrictions will improve the presentation of analysis and will prevent inappropriate evaluations. The first and most obvious constraint in most cases is money; after this, the list becomes hazy. Constraints do not have to be physical or even measurable, but they do have to be recognized.

One constraint that must be considered early in the analysis is top management's philosophy toward scientific management. The perfect solution to an important problem could be arrived at through systems analysis, and yet never be implemented because of top management's distrust (or fear) of scientific management. Other constraints are psychological, sociological, technical, traditional, administrative, political, and, of course, physical (personnel and equipment).

The definition of criteria is important to the analyst, for these are the rules or standards by which he or she ranks the alternatives in order of desirability. They must be relevant to the problem area, include consideration of all major effects relative to the objectives, and, ideally, be adaptable to meaningful quantification. It is important to remember that, in some cases, the mere mention that analysis is being undertaken or action is under consideration may be enough impetus to significantly alter the problem situation.

The collection of data is somewhat mundane and even boring, but it is obviously as important as any other part of the analysis. It is mandatory that all pertinent data relating to each alternative be collected in a usable format, and by a method that will not bias the solution.

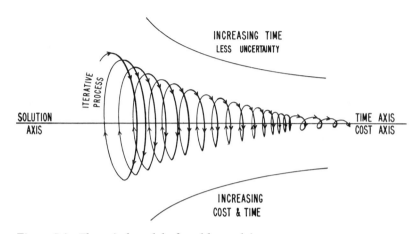

Figure 5.1   The spiral model of problem solving

Building a model is not always necessary in every analysis, but in complex problems for which a vast amount of data exists for each, a model is generally needed because experimenting with the real system is either impossible, economically infeasible, or quite dangerous, as in some defense projects. A model can also serve as an aid to thought and communication, a tool for production, and an aid for control purposes and for training and instruction.

The evaluation of the alternatives is the "putting everything together" step. This can be done through many analytical tools, using the predetermined criterion as a measuring stick. Two of the most publicized evaluation methods are cost-benefit analysis and cost-effectiveness analysis. In cost-benefit analysis, the cost of implementing each alternative is compared with the dollar value of the benefits accrued from implementation. Cost-effectiveness analysis compares the cost of implementation of each alternative with its real benefit.

The Decision-making Steps

Following the basic steps of systems analysis, the decision maker should perform a final check to answer the following kinds of questions: *Were the objectives of the problem stated correctly? Has the data changed? Are there any new assumptions or constraints?* It is possible to expend considerable time performing this final check or review, but in practical management situations the decision maker has to come up with a timely solution for implementation. The constraints defined, specifically time and money, normally will not allow the decision maker to follow the well-known theoretical problem-solving model to the perfect solution with no uncertainty (see Figure 5.1).

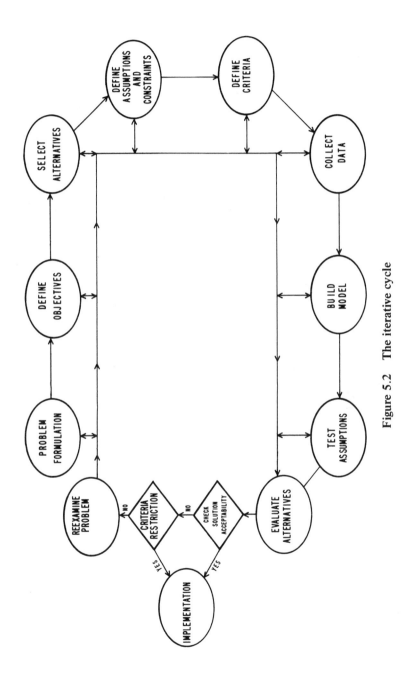

Figure 5.2   The iterative cycle

After the analyst has evaluated the alternatives, the decision maker must identify the best solution by considering facts, assumptions, and uncertainties for the problem. In certain situations, the systems analyst and the decision maker are the same person, but usually the analysis is performed by someone on the staff of the decision maker.

If the alternative identified is considered acceptable by the decision maker, the plan is implemented; if it is not acceptable, the decision maker must evaluate the constraints in order to determine if time and/or money is available to continue in the iterative model, as shown in Figure 5.2. In many cases, the decision maker may be forced to implement a less than optimal plan. As implied earlier, the constraints placed on the analyst are frequently so restrictive that the solution is often nothing better than an "intelligent guess."

Something should be said about what systems analysis is *not*. It is not a panacea for every decision maker. It does not tell the decision maker which alternative to choose. It is a method of investigating, not solving, problems. All of the various components of the analysis are defined by humans and often based on many untested assumptions. A correct decision cannot be assured even if the analysis is carried out to perfection.

Importance of Quality Decision Making

New Constraints

The constraints imposed upon the decision maker are often subtle and troublesome. Although there were many constraints imposed upon the decision makers of the early 1900s, they are not comparable with those that have been added during recent years.

As labor unions grew in strength, management found that it could no longer assume that its employees were just another resource to be utilized in the production process. Any decision involving the labor force has to be scrutinized to ensure that a contract has not been broken. There have been many examples in which an entire factory has been closed down by a strike called because one worker was fired. Government legislation such as the Occupational Safety and Health Act, which requires an employer to assure that employees have safe and healthy work environments, requires improved decision making. The spiraling cost of labor in itself is enough to warrant the careful analysis of all alternatives.

"Consumerism" has come to light in the past few years, obliging industry to recognize its responsibility to its customers. Regulatory agencies, formerly puppets of the industries they regulated, have found new strength and courage in the public outcry for better and safer products. Most states have product liability laws that strongly favor the consumer.

Since the end of World War II and the introduction of television, the vastness of the federal government has become more and more evident to the general public. The Department of Defense can no longer give out lavish contracts to researchers to develop weapon systems that might never be used. An agency or bureau can no longer hide major mistakes from the public. It is known in governmental circles that the public will view an area of government more critically if it discovers a major mistake within it. This is a great constraint placed on many governmental heads today.

The increasing public concern and environmental laws promoted most manufacturing industries to add pollution control equipment. However, much of the public wants environmental improvements without product price increases. Effective decision making will aid in the development of lower cost antipollution manufacturing operations.

These are some of the recent constraints placed upon the decision maker, and more will probably develop. Decisions cannot be made without knowing their full impact on the public as well as on the various markets.

Increased Number of Alternatives

Another area that has changed for the decision maker and complicated the decision process is the number of alternatives available to attain a certain objective. Recently, technology has moved so rapidly that no manager could possibly remain completely up-to-date, even in his or her own field. Of course, if the best alternative is not known, the decision maker can only make an inferior decision.

The other extreme (considering too many alternatives) is demonstrated by the fact that a new breed of professional has entered the scene—the consultant salesperson. In many cases, these people could be called "alternative creators." Without a systematic method to evaluate all of the various alternatives presented, the decision maker may choose an alternative that fulfills the consultant's objectives, but not the organization's. Things are complicated even further when a computer is a possible component of some or all of the alternatives.

It is difficult to imagine a complex decision that does not involve the services of a computer, either as part of an alternative or in the analysis of the alternatives. To a decision maker not knowledgeable in the computer field, the various design alternatives incorporating computer technology can boggle the mind. But this should not cause rejection of the computer, because it can both improve some alternatives and expedite the analysis.

The basic factor to remember is that the computer is just another tool by which the analyst or decision maker obtains the desired objectives. Also, a computer salesperson who begins to describe the various characteristics of hardware and software systems is talking about means and not ends. The computer specialist who begins the conversation by asking what output is needed or what objectives are sought is the person who is going to help.

Time is a constraint in most decisions. In a marketplace where fad products may have a life cycle of 6 months, or in a world where total destruction could be complete within a day, a decision maker can ill afford not to take advantage of any tool that will speed up the decision-making process without adding uncertainty.

Summary

Systems analysis is a technique for structuring common sense in problem evaluation. Problems confronting decision makers have become more complex by the addition of new constraints such as pollution control, more stringent product liability laws, and a more observant public. In summary, the use of systems analysis will improve the decision maker's problem-solving capability. The following points should be remembered:

Systems analysis is (or should be) the documentation of a method for analyzing problems.

Systems analysis can be applied to many business areas outside the scientific/technological field.

Systems analysis is not a panacea; the decision maker must ultimately select and implement the best alternative.

Decision-making Techniques

Expected Value

The expected value decision-making technique is one that is used when the manager wishes to quantify the degree of uncertainty associated with each alternative problem solution.

Computations of expected value can take into account changes in the environment along with the subjective probability of the occurrence of each state. The expected value of an act is defined as the weighted average of all of the conditional values of the act, each conditional value being weighted by its probability, as shown in the following equation:

$$EV = \sum_{i=1}^{n} P(S_i)W_i$$
$$= P_1(S_1)W_1 + P_2(S_2)W_2 + \cdots + P_n(S_n)W_n$$

where

EV = expected value

$P(S_i)$ = probability of occurrence of state i

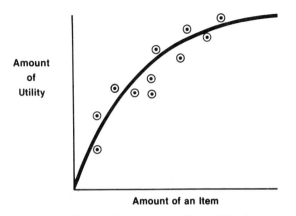

Amount of an Item

Figure 5.3   General form of a typical utility function

W_i = worth of outcome under the ith state of nature

n = total number of outcomes under consideration

An example of the application of the expected value technique is the estab-lishment of production levels by means of a sales forecast. Mr. Smith, general manager of a fast-food factory located in a small midwestern town, wants to forecast sales for the next year. He believes sales are determined mostly by personal income levels in the region. In accordance with expected value terms, the various income levels are states of nature. Mr. Smith thinks that four states of nature are possible: First, that incomes will decrease by 2 percent. Second, that incomes will not change. Third, that incomes will rise by 3 percent. Fourth, that incomes will rise by 8 percent. To these states he estimates the probabilities as 0.10, 0.30, 0.50, and 0.10, respectively. Lastly, he considers that the out-comes (sales levels for the next year) for the four states of nature are $1 million, $1.3 million, $1.9 million, and $2.5 million, respectively.

The expected value may be computed as follows:

EV = (0.10) ($1,000,000) + (0.30) ($1,300,000)

= + (0.50) ($1,900,000) + (0.10) ($2,500,000) = $1,690,000

The expected sales level of $1,690,000 is based on Mr. Smith's estimate of the probabilities and worth outcomes of each state of nature.

Utility

The utility decision-making technique is used when management wants to include personal values in the consideration of each alternative. Utility is defined as the power to satisfy human wants. The utility of an outcome is the subjective preferences placed upon the outcome and is usually measured in dimensionless units. For example, consider any desirable "item." Most people prefer more rather than less, but at a decreasing rate. For a given item or outcome an individual's utility function can be constructed by plotting units of utility (personal perference) against the amount of the item the individual possesses, as shown in Figure 5.3. In situations comparing more than one alternative, the technical manager should select the alternative with the maximum utility.

An example of a management decision involving the utility technique is sales forecasting. The XYZ Corporation produces product A. The sales forecaster consults with the sales manager and they decide that the four most likely levels of sales for next year are $40 million, $35 million, $30 million, and $25 million. These four levels were developed in light of assumptions regarding the level of engineering for product design and manufacturing, consumer acceptance of the brand, actions of competitors, and retailer merchandising and promotion efforts. Furthermore, a minimum level of sales has been estimated. This is the magnitude that would be achieved if most or all of the factors determining sales-consumer desires and incomes, competitive activities, and so on operated adversely but within reason. For product A this minimum level is $10 million. Utility relationships could be developed for each projected sales level based on the manager's value of sales dollars above $10 million.

Summary

A decision is the selection of the preferred course of action from two or more alternatives, and is completed under known or uncertain conditions. Decisions may be classified as programmed (well structured and routine) or nonprogrammed for more complex issues. The systems analysis approach structures a methodology for decision making and is recommended for technical managers. Following problem definition with assumptions and constraints, data is collected and analyzed through model development to formulate various alternatives. The final decision (alternative selection) may utilize expected value and utility theory to compute the cost-benefit or cost-effectiveness for each alternative.

Notes

1. H. A. Simon, *The New Science of Management Decisions,* Harper & Row, New York, 1960.

2. R. L. Shell and D. F. Stelzer, Systems Analysis: Aid To Decision Making. *Business Horizons,* vol. 14, no. 6, December 1971, pp. 67-72.

6 Individuals and Groups: Their Needs and Behavior

Development of Human Needs

As the basis for understanding employee behavior and its impact on management within organizations, one must understand both employee needs and organizational needs. Individual needs develop slowly from childhood, but organizational needs can change quickly and unexpectedly. Since these two sets of needs develop from different bases and may assume different characteristics, it is easy to see why conflict often develops between organizational and individual needs. Individual needs begin with early childhood and, as infants progress gradually into adulthood, their needs tend to take on a particular configuration. Variations exhibited in this configuration can be seen in the unique personalities among individuals. Professor Chyris Argyris, in his classic book, *Personality and Organization,* which was published in the late 1950s, discussed the development of personality from infancy to adulthood that characterized the normal adult and a different personality configuration that characterized the normal child.[1] An analysis of Argyris' approach provides considerable insight with regard to adult needs in organizational life. Specifically, Argyris pointed out that adults have a need for superordination and control over their environment. Related to this need the normal adult is characterized by independence, decisiveness, and a realistic time perspective of personal and environmental events.

The categorization of needs that is most commonly used in organizational behavior courses, professional development seminars, and in-house company training programs is Abraham Maslow's Hierarchy of Needs.[2] While this particular model is also discussed in Chapter 8 on motivation, it is important to note here that Maslow identified five basic needs: physiological, security, social, ego, and self-actualization. As can be seen in Figure 6.1, Maslow arranged these needs in a hierarchy, with the lower needs taking on predominant importance; once satisfied, the next level of needs assumes greater importance.

Order of priority of human needs

Figure 6.1 Abraham Maslow's Hierarchy of Needs

Most organizational research tends to support the conclusion that the lower level needs are largely satisfied in organizational endeavors, and this conclusion is most appropriate for managerial and professional employees.[3] Specifically, one's needs for food, clothing, shelter, and safety are taken care of by minimum wage legislation, sustained periods of prosperity, and, of course, governmental regulations regarding health and safety. Although technical managers should recognize that all employees have these needs, and that they are vitally important to the well being of their subordinates, in a management sense these needs are often of minimal importance because they are largely satisfied. Also, a given employee's ability to gain friends in an organizational environment tends to be an attainable goal, and social needs are usually quite well satisfied.

Applications of Research Findings on Needs for Technical Management

Many behavioral scientists believe that higher level needs should be of major concern to practicing managers. These needs revolve around the Maslow grouping that includes self-esteem and self-actualization, namely, status, esteem, and recognition. Studies show that blue collar workers often attach more importance to lower level needs than do professionally oriented employees such as engineers, scientists, and managers. Occupation seems to have more to do with the prioritization of need satisfaction than does income or level of accomplishment.[4] These findings are particularly important in view of the significance attached to the organizational environment and an employee's need to achieve.

Needs for certain goal realization, e.g., achievement, power, and affiliation, have emerged from a useful projection technique called the Thematic Apperception Test (TAT) developed by H. A. Murray. The TAT consists of 20 pictures that are presented to a given subject who is asked to explain the events in the pictures, and often a varying configuration of needs for power, affiliation, and achievement as well as other needs clearly emerge in that explanation.

Needs for power, affiliation, and achievement have been investigated by several prominent behavioral scientists such as David McClelland who has analyzed the need for achievement. According to McClelland, a person's desire to do things better is due to a specific motivation to achieve, and this motivation is acquired rather than genetic and can be taught.[5] It has been found that successful professional people tend to score high in achievement. Since achievement motivation is learned, organizational conditions are important to its development. For example, engineering and scientific managers should know that high achievers prefer challenging work and periodic feedback on their performance.[6]

Each individual has a unique need pattern. One employee may be strong in the social affiliation configuration, but relatively weak in the power need element. Another employee may have a high need for achievement, but much less need for affiliation with others. A knowledge of these factors is important in selecting, placing, and motivating employees in the engineering and scientific environment.

While individuals are unique in their need structure, there are similarities among individuals. Generally speaking, most organizational environments are competitive, and they often establish reward systems that provide greater opportunities for achievement, prestige, power, and social development among those who do well. This provision is one of the bases for the modern approaches to motivation that will be discussed in Chapter 8. However, in order to understand basic organizational behavior, it is important to point out that these approaches are based on a common knowledge of the content of specific needs, the significance of these needs to individual employees, and the fact that the organization plays a major part in satisfying these needs.

Causes of Conflict Between Employees and Organizations

While an organization can have a profound impact on the development of individual needs and the realization of high levels of self-esteem, many organizations do not respond to individual needs favorably, and often create a considerable amount of frustration to these needs, and conflict results. A quick review of organizational purpose yields considerable insight as to why such a conflict often exists. First, most organizations are rational. They have a specific purpose toward which they are directed which usually focuses on a profit-making or efficiency objective; consequently, organizations operate most effectively if behavior is kept on a prescribed course. As a result employees are often put in a confining situation. Their freedom must be restricted if the organization is to move toward goal attainment, and work assignments are not necessarily conducive to individual development or perceived by employees as supportive of their own specific needs. This situation results in the conflict between individual needs and organizational needs that Argyris developed some twenty years ago.[7] Several current authors believe that we have made little progress in alleviating this type of conflict; namely, organizations in general have not developed the kinds of jobs and promoted the freedom that will allow for individual self-expression and individual need satisfaction, particularly for higher level needs. Two common explanations for this problem reside in fundamental characteristics of modern organizations: First, the chain-of-command principle which places a subordinate under the control of one superior, and, secondly, task specialization which has become so prevalent in manufacturing firms and has wielded its way into most other types of enterprise. The presence of these factors tends to make employees feel inferior and frustrated.

In the environment of engineering and scientific organizations, this particular type of conflict can be severe. Engineering and professional staff groups generally tend to be well educated, and consequently are concerned with the ego and status needs that have been expressed by so many prominent behavioral scientists. They seek recognition for good work, and a relatively free environment in which they can set out to attain or achieve that recognition.[8] There is much evidence in the literature to support the conclusion that many environments do not provide this freedom or the much-needed recognition. Consequently, many of these professional groups become frustrated and devote a considerable amount of energy to activities which are designed to deal with frustration at the expense of organizational effectiveness. In view of the significant impact of the organizational environment upon individual needs, satisfaction, and the prevalent importance of the interaction of the individual with the organization, is is useful to look more closely at the organizational environment as it impacts on individual behavior.

Culture and Status

Cultural patterns significantly influence both individual behavior and the organizational environment. Culture can be defined as the value systems or modes of behavior to which people in a given geographical area subscribe. Thus, by definition, country boundaries would offer the clearest example of cultural differentiation. The individual behavioral patterns and the organizational environment found in Japan are quite different than those exhibited in the United States. The Japanese system, which is an outgrowth of feudalism that characterized Japan in the early part of this century, clearly supports the welfare concept and yields a paternalistic type of management that has proven to be successful among Japanese firms. On the other hand, the competitive educational system and the values traditionally taught American children by their parents for achievement and recognition have made it difficult for paternalistic patterns of management to work in the United States. This fact is particularly true in engineering and research environments because the employees who staff these types of organizations are an outgrowth of systems where competitiveness and recognition have been fundamentally characteristic.

Subculture

Subculture differences within any given set of country boundaries also impact on corporate environments and individual behavior. Work patterns in unionized urban areas are quite different than those patterns demonstrated in nonunionized rural areas in the United States. For example, management practices that work well in the Chicago area may fail in small cities in the southeast. Due to the impersonal environment of the urban area with its large number of unionized industrial workers, effectiveness is improved if paternalism is minimized by supervisors. Specific channels of appeal through union grievance procedures or the application of specific bureaucratic rules by supervisors is more acceptable to urban employees. Managers are also expected to be "tough but fair." Conversely, in rural areas less characterized by strong unionization and impersonality, informal appeals and emphasis on company loyalty by supervisors may work quite well. Technical managers with strong success records may find it necessary to apply different management styles in accordance with subcultural variations.

Social Structure

An analysis of culture alone is insufficient to gain an understanding of the complexity of the broader organizational environment. Each organization is a part of the broader social structure of a given culture, such as within the United States. Its position within that structure has a certain amount of significance attached to it through the employees and clients who deal with the organization. Because organizations occupy a definite place in the social structure, they are able to afford specific positions with regard to prestige and performance to individual employee members. Each position in the organization carries with it certain expectations with regard to performance, status, and privileges that accrue to the incumbent. A set of expectations becomes a defined role for the incumbent. More rigid expectations result in a more clearly defined role for the individual employee. The significance of this fact to technical managers is that many employees are responding to what they regard as the proper role for their job or the jobs of others, rather than expressing their true feelings about performance, supervision, or interaction with employee or client groups.

Perception

Another important variable related to roles and expectations in the organizational environment is perception. Perceptions relate not only to how we see the world around us (and in this case, the organizational environment), but to how we see ourselves. A position in a job hierarchy coupled with the place that the organization may occupy in the broader social structure has a very important impact on how incumbents in a given position see themselves and their corporate environment, and how other organizational members see and relate to them as employees. Important to the technical manager is the fact that engineering and scientific people in an organization may clearly be differentiated from nonengineering and nonscientific employees by the majority of other organizational members or clients. When this situation occurs, it specifically affects the complexity of the managerial task. For example, often the engineering manager also supervises other nonengineers or nonprofessional support staff. Because of differing perceptions, there may be communication problems among the subordinates precipitated by feelings of favoritism or a lack of understanding of each other's jobs that substantially reduces effectiveness within the organizational unit. Engineers may be perceived as occupying a very rigidly defined role which results in narrow applications of technology to job tasks, and communication may not be as open with other groups as is needed.

The effective engineering and scientific manager who also supervises other groups must try to break down these narrow perceptions by realistically reflecting the expanding role of today's engineer and scientist. This will help to dispel charges or perceptions of favorable treatment toward the engineering group, and thereby increase the general level of cooperation among all subordinates.

The engineering manager's task is more complex when the span of management includes nonengineering support personnel. Although their needs may not be as highly developed, nonengineering professionals have the same needs for self-expression, independence, and recognition as engineers. If engineers and scientists are perceived to be getting greater opportunities for freedom and advancement because of favoritism, managerial problems will be intensified.

Some organizations have effectively dealt with this problem by separating scientific, research and development, and specialized engineering groups from the rest of the corporate staff. Often there is a different geographical location, or if this is impractical, a separate building may be allocated to these special groups at the corporate site. Since both of these solutions may be too costly for many organizations and impractical in small ones, strong interpersonal skills are particularly useful to engineering managers in these latter situations.

Status

Status, which has one of the strongest influences on individual behavior in the organizational environment, may be defined as a hierarchical ranking or ordering of people in a given society. According to Chester Barnard, there are three conditions that determine one's status in an organizational environment.[9] These conditions are as follows: First, the differences in the abilities of the individuals; second, the differences in the difficulties of doing various kinds of work; and third, the differences in the importance of various kinds of work. All three of these conditions are involved in determining status. Since the work that is done must be perceived by others as being important, the presence of superior ability or doing a job of extreme difficulty does not necessarily provide one with high status.

In looking at these variables, it is important to note that status is something given to an individual by others. Since status is given or earned and outside the control of the employee, it cannot be demanded successfully. In our culture, status is highly valued by individuals, and is usually associated with the nature of employee jobs and positions. Since it is so highly valued by employees, it is an important determinant of behavior and is vigorously protected. For example, changes in the organizational environment that threaten the status of an individual employee will be vehemently resisted (see Chapter 10). Likewise, communications from managers or others that are perceived to be threatening to the status of an individual employee also will be resisted (see Chapter 7).

Employees attempt to protect their status position by exhibiting behavior purposely designed to influence others to perceive their work as being difficult and important, and they resist all kinds of communication that downgrade the importance of their work or the abilities they possess. Technical managers need to understand that status and recognition are vitally important to these types of employee groups. Studies indicate that status is an important motivator among lower level scientists.[10] Also, pay and status must be commensurate with achievement, and the technical manager should give careful attention to the impact of specific rewards on individual status. One study showed that scientists who are underrecognized by the organization relative to perceived achievement by colleagues are more likely to leave their jobs.[11]

Engineers and scientists will resist activities by management that downgrade the importance of their work or reflect adversely on their abilities as individual contributors to the organizational effort. Also, they will tend to resist actions by management that tend to suggest that nonprofessionally oriented employees that work around them are of equal status or importance to the organization in the jobs that they do. It is usually true that managers can support the status systems of professional engineering-type personnel and build a more effective team by differentiating these groups from others and reinforcing their status positions. Differentiating the professional is often accepted by nonprofessionally oriented employees because of the varying sets of expectations that determine the roles for their respective occupations. Nonprofessional employees have a different set of expectations with regard to themselves and the employees around them. They often do not perceive themselves as being as high in status as a professionally oriented employee, and will accept differential treatment that supports this perception. On the other hand, professionally oriented employees, such as engineers, do not have this perception, and they become very resistant to attempts to put them on an equal status basis with a nonprofessional employee.

Status Congruency

Status congruency exists when the perceptions that two or more employees have toward each other are mutually supportive. Examples of status congruency are as follows: Individual A perceives individual B as a peer; B also perceives A as a peer—or as a second example, A perceives B as a superior, and B perceives A as a subordinate. In each of these two examples the individuals are on the same wavelength in their relative status perceptions of each other. When people of perceived lower status are given symbols and insignia to indicate higher status by management, this simply serves to decrease status congruence in the organization and promote ineffectiveness.

W. F. Whyte's classic study of the restaurant indicates a very interesting aspect of status relationships and organizational life, which has direct applicability to engineering and professional managers. Whyte found that people behave toward others in a direct relationship to their status perceptions with regard to themselves versus others.[12] People of perceived higher status will resist orders from peers and people of perceived lower status; consequently, organizational efficiency is decreased to the extent that status relationships are not congruent with the decision-making process in the organizational environment. Additional research concerning status relationships supports their relevance to the level of effectiveness of the organizations studied.[13]

There are many symbols that are indicative of one's status in an organization, such as size and location of the employee's office, number of support personnel, administrative or occupational titles, rate of pay, and even the number of buttons on the telephone. More effective managers use status symbols to support existing relationships, namely, to promote status congruence within the organization. The technical manager should understand the perceived status relationships that exist within an organization, and reinforce those relationships that promote organizational effectiveness.

Summary

Culture, social structure, expectations and role, and status work hand in hand to weave the complex environment of the engineering and scientific organization. These factors coupled with the very complex and unique set of needs associated with individual employees must be understood by the effective technical manager. There is a continuous interaction between individual needs and the organizational environment which, in fact, determines the effectiveness and the efficiency of that management system.

Emergence and Significance of Informal Groups

Intense conflict between individuals and the organization can often be minimized if employees become an integral part of a colleagial group of fellow workers. There is a natural tendency for employees who see each other regularly or have common friends or associates who see each other quite frequently to develop a close relationship which is defined as an informal group. Groups are an outgrowth of common employee needs. Needs for understanding, identification with one's self and others, support and friendship, and security are the more prevalent needs that stimulate group development.[14] Groups usually are spontaneous because they are an outgrowth of these needs. When an employee is frustrated because of an environment that is impeding personal need satisfaction, and that environment is fostered by an upper level management which this particular employee cannot influence, it is natural to engage in group activity.

Dealing with these common informal groups is an important aspect of engineering and scientific management, and the understanding of their behavior can contribute very directly to the effectiveness or ineffectiveness of the organization. Groups constitute greater threats to management efficiency and effectiveness than do individuals. They can either upset or enhance cooperation with the organization because they can facilitate or reduce motivation among their members.

Groups can take three stances with regard to management. First, a positive stance, which supports management activity. Second, a negative stance, which involves working against management activity and goals. And third, a neutral stance, namely, not really impacting positively or negatively on organizational goals. Stances are best seen as part of a continuum as shown in Figure 6.2, with group behavior occurring at any given point on the continuum depending on the time and situation. The ideal managerial situation is to have informal groups support management's activities and goals by increasing the level of cooperation.

Nature of Informal Group Control

Groups play a very important facilitative role in enforcing a given stance simply because they have control over the relative level of need satisfaction for certain

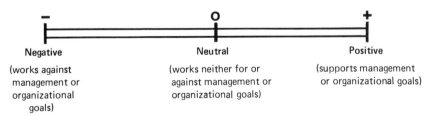
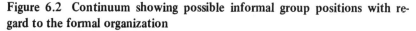

Figure 6.2 Continuum showing possible informal group positions with regard to the formal organization

important needs of their membership. As indicated previously, members of the organization are particularly concerned with protection, understanding, warmth, support, friendship, and security. Groups can substantially enhance or reduce the satisfaction of these needs within the organization. Denial of group membership, privileges, or support can be very positive factors in lowering the sense of security, belonging, or identification for individual employees. Ostracism and denial of group privileges is an important factor in the control of individual behavior which is under the influence of the group.

Importance of Group Cohesion

The group's ability to impose sanctions, such as ostracism, is partially dependent upon the cohesiveness of the membership of the group. Cohesiveness is the strength of the bonds among the membership or the relative tightness of the bonds within the group. Cohesiveness is the function of three basic factors: First, the prestige of the group. Second, the availability of membership in other groups in the same general environment. Third, the strength of the informal leadership within the group. Informal or emergent leadership is usually assumed by a member of the group that most clearly identifies with the norms and values of the group as a whole, and as a result, is supportive of what the group wants to do.

If the group is high status relative to other adjacent groups, or if none exist to bid for its membership, and the group has an emergent leader with strong leadership qualities who embodies the values that the group membership supports as a whole, the ingredients are present for a cohesive group which can be very powerful in enforcing its codes of behavior. Membership in that group will be desired, and the leadership function will be sufficiently strong to enable the group members to carry out their objectives and maintain a liaison with each other. This type of group can be a powerful force in determining the effectiveness of the management. If the group has these characteristics but assumes a negative stance, management can have endless problems in trying to sustain cooperation and motivate its employees. Conversely, management will have one of its strongest allies if the group is cohesive and strong, and members are convinced that managerial and group goals are similar and mutually desirable. In this case the technical manager has a valuable tool to increase motivation, cooperation, reduce conflict, and raise the overall level of effectiveness of the particular unit. This is a major element of sound management practice in engineering and scientific organizations.

Groups with a negative or neutral stance can often be converted to a positive stance within the organization. This conversion is part of the important task of management. Converting groups that are neutral or negative to a positive position will significantly increase the effectiveness of the organization. Several management practices are useful in accomplishing this task.

Specifically, it is important for the technical manager to be able to identify and work with the informal leadership of the group in question. Most every group has some leadership function, and sometimes this is complicated by the fact that it is performed by more than one individual. Usually leadership changes from one individual to another when a situation changes, but often these situations can be categorized. For example, one particular group member may be a leader in dealing with complaints and conflicts with management, and a different individual may be the leader in imposing sanctions and control on the group's behavioral patterns. A third individual may emerge as group leader when crises situations arise where immediate behavioral change is necessary. Technical managers should understand this complex leadership process and be able to identify particular leaders in given situations, so they can consult with them when consultation would be both beneficial and desirable. Managers should realize that negative stances are strengthened in direct proportion to the inability of management to identify and solve problems of individual employees. As indicated earlier in this chapter, the more workers are frustrated with management's failure to respond to their needs, the more the seeds of a strong group, which will probably assume a negative stance, have been sown by the management. Thus, if the management can work directly with individuals to release employee frustration, they have made significant progress in minimizing their problems with groups. Technical managers will help attain these desirable ends by designing jobs that will be stimulating and rewarding, and providing a monetary and need-satisfying reward system that recognizes good performance. The extent that management is able to take active steps to provide these rewards will relate directly to their ability to build a more effective results-oriented team.

In dealing with groups it is important to understand that management cannot eliminate the group as long as a liaison is taking place among employees. Sometimes managers make the mistake of trying to shut off communication among group members, isolate group members, or engage in other similar activities hoping to eliminate group presence. This course of action is generally unwise because it will only serve to reinforce the membership's belief that management is not supportive, but exploitive. The impact of this perception will be to strengthen the group bonds among members and in some instances force group activities to go "underground." Underground activities are simply destructive group behavioral patterns, such as sabotage, which are purposely done in a very secretive manner. Such activities are difficult to discern directly by management; therefore, pinpointing responsibility for negative consequences is difficult, so corrective action is delayed. When group bonds are strengthened from a negative action by management, the end result usually will be a negative impact upon the goals and effectiveness of the organization.

Groups in Engineering and Scientific Organizations

Studies show that groups in engineering and professionally oriented organizations are as prevalent as in manufacturing or other types of organizations.[15] Similarities in the presence of groups among organizational types is explained by the nature of groups. Groups usually are formed because of spontaneity of contacts, a common need which results in a common bond, and some kind of shared interest in particular organizational outcomes. These conditions are shared by individuals who work for the same manager or perform a common task. Thus, the nature of the supervision and/or nature of the task have major influences on the composition, size, and cohesiveness of the group. Professionals are commonly bound together by similar tasks, and they will group with each other accordingly. Research laboratories and other professional environments often have concentrated supervision which has a direct impact on the needs of scientific or engineering employees. Common supervision provides the catalyst for group development and tends to set definite boundaries on the size and membership of the group itself.

Sometimes technical personnel will purposely limit their scope of behavior and develop what is commonly called a conservative type of work group in dealing with the management. This is particularly true when these professionals possess unique skills which, because of their education, training, and experience with a given firm, cannot be replaced easily from the outside. If these skills are vital to the overall objectives of the management, these groups are potentially strong. Engineers in particular are quick to realize that they maintain considerable power as a group, and although one of them might easily be replaced, the entire group of engineers simply cannot be replaced in short-run situations. These types of engineering groups often have highly centralized leadership, but they have restrained pressure tactics which are used for the attainment of specific objectives. They are difficult for management to deal with because management realizes that failure to cooperate with them can be extremely costly to the organization. In fact, management must respond to the specific demands of the group because of the high costs associated with losing group cooperation.

It is essential that managers of skilled engineering professional groups attempt to identify potential problem areas before they surface into major conflicts, and try to smooth the path to need satisfaction and goal attainment for group members. The engineering manager who fails at this effort will likely be managing a group that assumes a definitive negative stance against the organization. Periodic group meetings with subordinates where differences can be aired and acted upon by management are helpful for sustaining group support. However, these meetings should not be held too frequently and work best when they are conducted for a known purpose or in response to specific employee needs. The engineering manager should also have an agenda for each meeting which will help to generate results that are meaningful to the employees.

As will be discussed extensively in Chapter 11, management by objectives is one of the current useful tools available to bring groups together for a common objective, namely, the cooperation and attainment of goals for the organization. MBO permits the manager to involve the group, and as Professor Rensis Likert says, "to develop management by group objectives."[16] This is an essential element of the Likert System IV process of management, which is heavily oriented toward getting the group to become an integral part of the formulation, development, and attainment process with regard to organizational objectives. It is important to note that the attainment process is a critical element in group behavior because groups will often determine the number of objectives that are achieved. MBO enables a manager to automatically integrate the formulation and attainment aspect of management into the group structure, which will certainly enhance the probability that the attainment of important objectives will be an end result.

Notes

1. Chyris Argyris, *Personality and Organization,* Harper & Brothers, New York, 1957, p. 50.

2. Abraham H. Maslow, A Theory of Human Motivation. *Psychological Review,* vol. 50, 1943, pp. 370-396.

3. Mason Haire, Edwin E. Ghiselli, and Lynam Porter, Cultural Patterns in the Role of the Manager. *Industrial Relations,* February 1963, p. 113.

4. William E. Rief, Intrinsic Versus Extrinsic Rewards: Resolving the Controversy. *Human Resource Management,* Summer 1975, pp. 2-10.

5. D. C. McClelland, That Urge to Achieve. *Think,* vol. 32, no. 6, November-December 1966, pp. 19-23.

6. *Ibid.*

7. Argyris, *Personality and Organization.*

8. Donald C. Pelz and Frank M. Andrews, *Scientists in Organizations,* University of Michigan Institute for School Research, Ann Arbor, Mich., 1976, p. 8.

9. Chester I. Barnard, Functions of Status Systems in Formal Organizations, in W. F. Whyte (ed.), *Industry and Society,* McGraw-Hill, New York, 1946, pp. 46-70.

10. Pelz and Andrews, *Scientists in Organizations,* p. 111.

11. *Ibid.*

12. William F. Whyte, The Social Structure of the Restaurant. *American Journal of Sociology,* vol. 54, January 1949, pp. 302-308.

13. R. L. Stogdill, E. L. Scott, and W. E. Jaynes, Leadership and Role

Expectations, Research Monograph no. 86, Ohio State University Bureau of Business and Economic Research, Columbus, Ohio, 1956.

14. Leonard R. Sayles and George Strauss, *Human Behavior in Organizations,* Prentice-Hall, Englewood Cliffs, N.J., 1966, p. 83.

15. Mark Abrahamson, Informal Groups in the Research Laboratory. *Research/ Development,* April 1965, pp. 29-32.

16. Rensis Likert, Human Resource Accounting: Building and Assessing Productive Organizations. *Personnel,* May-June 1973, pp. 8-24.

7

Building Effective Communication

Importance of Achieving Good Communication

Many of the surveys done in recent years asking managers to prioritize the importance of problems that confront them today report that communication ranks number one. Communication makes the organization work. It determines the direction that the organization will take, impacts on both the motivational level of employees and the understanding that employees have of organizational purpose and goals. Communication, in essence, is the major determinant of the supervisory-subordinate relationship, and is a fundamental management task. Organizations that list responsibilities for their managers often list "communicating effectively" among the top five. Unfortunately, communication is so pervasive that it is often perceived as everybody's responsibility, and this fact dilutes the ability of management to pinpoint particular communication problems or deficiencies. The achievement of good communication is a complex and difficult managerial task, and this chapter will offer both analysis and insight designed to aid the technical manager in this process.

Formal and Informal Communication

There are two major types of communication within organizations, namely, formal and informal. Formal communications tend to be written down or are subject to a specific procedural design within the organizational context. Informal communications are usually oral, and they do not necessarily follow any procedural design or pattern of flow. Recent studies of communication pertinent to the engineering and scientific environment have revealed that oral communication is likely to be more current and efficient than formal written communication.[1] Most communications that flow from superior to subordinate are likely to be formal and are often transmitted in written form. Communications that move from subordinate to superior are usually informal and not written down. A considerable amount of all informal communication throughout the organization is commonly called the grapevine, which is a vitally important factor in determining the quantity and quality of transmitted information. Because of the importance of informal communication to the technical manager, additional attention will be given to both upward communication (subordinate to superior) and the grapevine in this chapter.

Dimensions of Communication

The three major dimensions of the communication process are downward, upward, and horizontal. While upward and horizontal communication are usually informal, downward communication is most frequently formal in nature. Both formal and informal communication are critically important for the organization to function effectively. Historically, the downward dimension has been given the most attention by researchers and practicing managers who have studied communication problems. Downward communication flows from superior to subordinate within the organization. As a practical matter, downward messages tend to be given the greatest attention by managers because without them the organization would cease to function.

The other side of downward communication is, of course, feedback or upward communication, namely, information flowing from subordinate to superior. A variety of researches over the last 30 years have indicated that upward communication is essential for downward communication to be effective, because the vital element of feedback is necessary for downward communication to be understood. Several studies also show that feedback is necessary for effective communication in the engineering and scientific environment.[2]

Unfortunately, even though much has been written about it, upward communication often gets little consideration from management. There are four principal reasons for this neglect:

1. Upward communication involves considerable time and energy on the part of management. For example, listening is very time consuming, and managers often feel too pressed to devote this extra time to listening to what employees have to say.

2. Upward communication may be perceived as threatening to managers, particularly if things are not going very well. As a result of this threat, managers often turn off to what is being said, and try to get employees to avoid talking about important work issues. Since individuals' normal tolerance for criticism is often low, they do not listen to what subordinates have to say when they feel that those messages may be containing personal criticism.

3. Subordinates often realize that managers resent criticism, and that they usually have some control over the well being of subordinates, such as promotions and pay raises. Subordinates are therefore often reluctant to talk to superiors about specific problems that might be interpreted as criticism because they realize that these things may be used against them by their managers.

4. The organization tends to design its information flow devices to support the managers' downward movement of communication, but the upward flow does not have equal support in terms of devices, e.g., secretarial assistance, staff support, or proximity of contact, so it is much more difficult for subordinates to get their messages across to higher level managers.

One-way Versus Two-way Communication

While the preceding points help explain why upward communication and feedback are neglected, research evidence continues to suggest that technical managers should make an extra effort to counteract these problems and assure that feedback flows freely. The authors have conducted experiments which illustrate this point using a popular diagrammed exercise at several management seminars attended by technical managers throughout the United States. In this exercise, participating managers are asked to draw interconnected rectangles on the basis of explanations made by a group leader who stands in front of the group.

Two specific methods are used to explain two different sets of rectangles. In the first method, the communicator stands behind a movable blackboard or other barrier and describes the relationships among the rectangles without the aid of direct visual contact with the group. The group is not allowed to ask any questions of the leader or to make any verbal gestures that indicate either understanding or lack of understanding of the explanations being made. In the second method, the leader comes out from behind the blackboard and stands in front of the group to explain another set of specific rectangles. In this particular situation, the leader can invite questions from the group and the group can ask the leader questions at any point in the explanation. The first method is an example of communication without feedback, and the second method exemplifies communication with feedback.

Five basic conclusions regarding effective managerial communication can be drawn from the results of this exercise:

1. Participating technical managers overwhelmingly prefer two-way communication with feedback to the one-way method.

2. Communication accuracy measured in terms of the number of participants who draw the rectangles correctly is much improved when feedback is present.

3. There is a general feeling of greater satisfaction with the work process when participation takes place.

4. While a majority of leaders prefer the democratic (feedback) method to the autocratic method (without feedback), a few leaders do not.

5. The democratic (feedback) method requires more time and is often perceived as a more difficult process by the leaders than the autocratic method (without feedback).

A closer look at the results of this exercise suggests several points of practical value to technical managers who wish to improve their communication skills. It clearly illustrates that feedback improves accuracy, morale, and general understanding of the intended message. However, it also shows that this understanding and accuracy is gained at some cost, namely, more time is involved. Thus, for very simple messages or messages where accuracy is not a critical problem, it may be desirable to use one-way methods of communication because they are more efficient timewise. Since a bigger percentage of communicators than receivers prefer the one-way method, there is an apparent tendency for many managers to use communication methods without feedback. Although the ability to understand communications is less without feedback, nonfeedback methods are quicker and easier. Also, in the absence of specific evidence, some managers incorrectly believe that communication without feedback is the most effective type.

While there are some situations that clearly call for communication without feedback, most managerial situations in the engineering and scientific environment require communication with feedback. This is particularly true when the nature of the information is complex, accuracy is important, and commitment by the subordinates is necessary or desirable. Very simple or trivial day-to-day communications are examples that do not warrant the extra time needed to include feedback or participation.

Communicating with the Scientist

In discussing the communication problems of scientists in business and industry, McLeod argues that these employee groups feel that originality, imagination, and freedom of expression are often discouraged in the corporate community.[3] These qualities are valued by scientists, but they are too frequently found only in university-oriented research teams. In fact, many scientists believe that status is only achieved by moving into managerial positions. Unfortunately, limited communication may actually tend to increase status as long as one remains a scientist, thus scientists may not communicate freely about their work. Whenever possible the scientific manager helps his subordinates blend their interests in pure research into the applied research needs of the company. In order to achieve this desirable goal, communication concerning pure or fundamental research should be supported and valued because these interests must be understood before effective integration with organizational needs can be attempted.

The Grapevine

The grapevine is an important part of informal communication. Understanding the nature and function of the grapevine is useful in developing effective communication skills. The grapevine is defined as the rumor mill or word-of-mouth information that is transmitted informally and at frequent intervals throughout the organization. Studies indicate that the grapevine operates very rapidly and is effective in spreading news through the organization.[4] It operates whenever employees get together, such as in lunch or snack areas, or during the contact that results from the regular performance of duties. Studies have shown that employees often expect to hear important managerial or organizational news by the grapevine rather than by any other method.[5] Official memoranda (one-way communication) from the supervisor are often ranked second or third. One study indicated that more grapevine sources were outside the employees' chain of command than within it, which indicates that the information passing through the grapevine came *around* management rather than *through* management.[6] It is also true that a considerable portion of communication among people within a given chain of command is of the informal grapevine type.

Making Constructive Use of the Grapevine

Since the technical manager cannot eliminate the grapevine, and since it is an important source of information to employees, it should be used effectively. The following points are particularly useful:

1. Don't withhold information that is important to subordinates for long periods of time based on the belief that they will not get this information until you decide to let them know about it, because the grapevine will probably get it to them extremely quickly. Information transmitted in this way will have a negative impact on your credibility, particularly if you deny the truthfulness of the information until a later date.

2. Information passing through the grapevine is often more acceptable to subordinates than information going directly through the chain of command. Thus, if a problem exists in getting a certain communication accepted, it is often useful to move it through the grapevine first, rather than by official announcement or memorandum.

3. Information received informally through grapevine channels should be assumed to be quite credible until proven otherwise. If this information

needs managerial action, it should be investigated quickly based on the assumption that it is truthful so action can be taken before major problems develop.

4. The grapevine should not be regarded as a liability, but an asset which can be constructively used to enhance the level of understanding within the organization.

Horizontal Communication

The third major dimension in the communications process is horizontal communication. Horizontal communication is usually informal and by definition takes place at peer levels, and is often one of the major ways that important problems are solved within the organization. The horizontal flow of communication is particularly important in technical staff and engineering operations because it enables engineers to pool knowledge in a professional group and improve their problem-solving ability. Although given less attention in the literature than the other two dimensions, horizontal communication is often very useful in professionally oriented groups to the emergence of problem-solving skills.

An environment that promotes feedback also encourages horizontal communication. Since managerial action that fosters the growth of both the upward and horizontal communication dimensions is desirable, the technical manager who engages in such activity can easily realize a double payoff.

Nonverbal Communication

While the content methods of communication are highly important, many studies indicate that nonverbal elements determine at least one-half of what is understood or heard in the communication process.[7]

Nonverbal communication requires "body expression" such as tone of voice, posture, facial expression, and eye contact while communicating messages in a verbal fashion to others. Tone of voice, eye contact, and posture have an impact on the ability of a communicator to get attention, establish credibility, and elicit feedback from subordinates. It is important to look at who you are speaking to, and to assume a posture that indicates attentiveness and importance being attached to what is being said. And finally, it is important to assume a tone of voice that emphasizes those elements of your communication that are regarded as essential. For example, a common criticism of certain teachers is that they talk in a monotone and everything comes out sounding the same. In any kind of communication, tone of voice should be purposely varied to emphasize those elements that are more important and deemphasize the elements that are less important. The time of day, minor work problems, or personal appearance should not be given the same emphasis as a primary work deficiency.

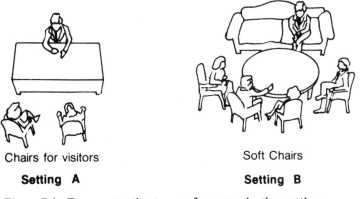

Chairs for visitors   Soft Chairs

Setting A   **Setting B**

Figure 7.1   Two contrasting types of communication settings

Seating arrangements and physical barriers in the communication setting have an important nonverbal effect on what is understood. When people sit across from each other with a table between them, they more often see the climate as competitive rather than cooperative. Once this barrier is removed and they sit adjacent to each other, e.g., at a round table, the environment is more likely to be seen as cooperative. Rapport is more easily established and upward communication flows more freely when physical barriers such as desks and tables do not exist between communicating parties.

It is desirable for a technical manager to have two types of seating arrangements in the office: one that contains a barrier, such as a desk, and one in which physical barriers do not exist. There are a few situations such as layoffs or transfers where it may be desirable to minimize feedback, and sitting behind a desk is useful. Conversely, in many instances feedback and rapport are essential, and in these cases being able to sit and talk more informally without physical barriers between the communicating parties is desirable. Figure 7.1 illustrates both types of communication settings. In setting A, the desk acts as a definite barrier which reduces feedback and rapport. In setting B, the sofa, low cocktail table, and soft chairs promote feedback and rapport.

It should be clear to the technical manager from the above analysis that a knowledge of the nature and impact of nonverbal communication can be directly applied to improve the level of understanding in the professional environment of engineering and scientific organizations.

Approaches to Improving Managerial Communication

In building an approach to improving communication within any given organizational unit, managers need to recognize the complexities of both the dimensions and types of communication. These managers should also take responsibility for the general level of communication within their respective organizational units. It is often desirable for a manager to conduct meetings with subordinates to discuss the problems of communication flow and find mutual solutions to these problems.

The number and type of meetings held should be carefully planned by the manager, because poorly planned meetings can do more harm than good. As Peter Drucker points out, an excess of meetings may indicate that jobs have not been properly defined or structured.[8] Many times the presence of a strong need to meet to solve problems suggests that the manager has failed to help plan, organize, and communicate job tasks effectively. Also, meetings conducted on short notice to solve crisis problems may not be perceived as purposeful by subordinates.

The Johari Window

The ability to communicate and to widen one's range of problem-solving potential is based in part on the willingness of the communicator to share knowledge, attitudes, and feelings with others. In fact, the extent to which we keep pertinent information about ourselves from others, or they keep information from us, reduces the level of two-way understanding. In order to better understand the impact of self-disclosure on understanding and problem solving, a pictorial view of this aspect of the communication process is shown in Figure 7.2. The Johari window is named after its developers, Joseph Luft and Harry Ingham, and gets its name because important elements of the communication process are depicted as containing four quadrants.[9] These four quadrants are the arena, blind spot, facade, and unknown areas. The arena is defined as the area where important facts about the communicator are known by both parties namely, the communicator and receiver. The blind spot is where important elements relating to the communicator are known by the receiver, but kept from the communicator. The facade is where some of these aspects are known by the communicator, but they are kept from the receiver. The unknown quadrant is where important information relating to the communicator is unknown by both parties. In order to be most effective, communication must take place where these important elements are known by both parties involved. Thus, in order to improve managerial communication, the technical manager should try to enlarge the arena whenever possible. The arena can be enlarged by reducing the blind spot, facade, or unknown areas. The facade is reduced by giving information about yourself, the blind spot is reduced by asking questions and getting information, and the unknown becomes known by exploring together with the receiver the elements of the communication that are not understood.

	Known by self	Not known by self
Known by others	**Arena** **I** I know these things about myself and so do you. Area of most meaningful communication	**Blind Spot** **II** You know things about me that I don't know
Not known by others	**Facade** **III** I know things about myself you don't know	**Unknown** **IV** Things I don't know about myself and you don't either

Figure 7.2 The Johari window [From *Group Processes: An Introduction to Group Dynamics* by **Joseph Luft** by permission of Mayfield Publishing Company (formerly National Press Books). Copyright © 1963, 1970 by Joseph Luft. See also *Of Human Interaction.*]

Using the Johari Window to Improve Organizational Communication

There are several practical messages from this communication model that should be understood by engineering and scientific managers. In order to get information from a subordinate, sometimes a manager must first provide information about himself, and this information may be personal in nature. This kind of information reduces the facade, which results in the subordinate becoming more willing to provide additional information to the manager. Useful information about the manager reduces the blind spot and improves understanding.

A valuable aid for the technical manager in both getting and receiving information is to be supportive to the people that provide such information. For example, if a manager gives personal or critical information about himself or herself which is not supported by the responses of the subordinate, it will be very difficult for the manager to release further information. Conversely, if the subordinate opens up and releases personal or critical information to the manager, but the manager either does not support this information or uses it to make the subordinate look bad, the communication process will break down. Specifically, the size of the arena will be reduced, and it will be more difficult to enlarge it in future communication.

Technical managers should support subordinates when they offer personal information, and at the same time educate subordinates on the importance of supporting others in order to establish rapport and build effective communication.

Another important aspect of the Johari window is the importance attached to being willing to ask questions and to explore unknown areas in the communication process. Often, good communication takes time, and managers should be willing to devote the time necessary to make communication effective, particularly on valuable matters to the organization. Experiments by social psychologists have shown that, in organizations characterized by status hierarchies, high and low status employees have difficulties communicating with each other. As pointed out in Chapter 6, studies show that status factors have a particularly strong impact on information flow in the engineering and scientific environment.

Thomas Allen reported on a series of studies conducted at the Sloan School of Management at the Massachusetts Institute of Technology, which conclude that few ideas flow into the laboratory directly from the scientific and technological literature. In one study, for example, only 15 percent of the idea generating messages could be attributed to the literature.[10] Outside or extraorganizational channels consistently performed more poorly than internal information channels in the provision of technical information. Lack of technical capability within the laboratory was often responsible for the decision to use outside sources.

When information must be attained on projects, it is often more useful to seek the capabilities within the organization than outside the organization. Studies of engineering groups have indicated that several sources rather than one single source often contribute to the discovery and formulation of a particular idea. It is common in a small laboratory to find that Ph.D.'s form a tightly knit group characterized by effective internal communication, but seldom discuss technical matters with non-Ph.D.'s. This type of clique behavior can disrupt organizational performance because communication and idea flow suffer. To solve this problem the technical manager should work to build a cooperative team that involves both the Ph.D.'s and non-Ph.D.'s.

One effective way to increase information flow and to build teamwork is for the manager to develop superordinate goals that draw both Ph.D.'s and non-Ph.D.'s together. Specifically, it is important to make laboratory Ph.D.'s see that helpful information from the non-Ph.D.'s may be very useful in attaining the basic goals of the organization. Attainment of these goals must result in rewards to both groups. This type of subordinate goal approach is valuable to both Ph.D. and non-Ph.D. groups, but it is most useful to focus it on the Ph.D. groups because usually the non-Ph.D. groups want to communicate with the higher status Ph.D.'s.

Finally, successful management of the communication process can be difficult for the engineering and scientific manager who supervises personnel with diverse educational backgrounds. Many of the points stressed throughout this chapter are useful to help resolve some of the group conflicts that can emerge. It should be clear that the successful development of team effort does not just happen; it requires strong and purposeful problem-solving action by technical managers.

Impact of Defensiveness on Understanding Messages

It is useful for each manager who is faced with problems of motivation, understanding, and morale to ask the following two questions. First, *what is it that I really want to accomplish in communicating with my subordinates?* Usually the answer to this question is, I want to correct deficiencies and move to keep the laboratory or overall organization on a prescribed course toward the attainment of specific goals. Additionally, I want to maintain or establish a collegial atmosphere among my staff. The second question then becomes, *what alternative is likely to yield this result most frequently?* Managers tend to agree that the answer to this question is the approach that will breed the lesser amount of defensiveness on the part of the receiver (subordinate). Defensiveness is defined as the process of defending one's self when threatened by a communication from others. Common examples of messages that cause defensiveness are those that are perceived to downgrade one's status or self-esteem.

Both the subordinate's and superior's ability to hear and understand is directly affected by the level of defensiveness that is present in the communications process. Jack Gibb has developed a sound approach to reducing the potential amount of defensiveness.[11] Gibb indicates that once an individual feels threatened either personally or as a group member by a communication, he or she will become defensive, and then all subsequent communication is directed at defending one's self and the true substance of the message is lost. Gibb points out the types of communication that breed defensiveness and proposes solutions to counteracting that defensiveness. Specifically, communication that is directed at personally evaluating or controlling the subordinate, or appears to communicate personal superiority to the subordinate by the superior, tends to breed defensiveness. Most employees become defensive when they feel they are being controlled or evaluated on a personal basis. Gibb maintains that these kinds of communication problems can, at least, partially be alleviated by more supportive techniques in communication.

Rather than communicating personal evaluation or control to the subordinate in problem situations, the manager should be descriptive and attempt to identify the problem with the subordinate. If done properly, this approach will develop an effective rapport and minimize the personal nature of any negative feedback or criticism that may be provided. For example, if a technical manager goes to a subordinate and says, "Bob, you are doing a lousy job, and you're getting our laboratory way behind in its scheduled development. I insist that you correct your problems immediately and move on a constructive course of action," it is apparent that the substance of this communication contains personal evaluation and has a control element in it directed at the subordinate. It is also clear that the subordinate will probably become defensive in his response to this particular type of communication. An alternative approach is as follows: "Bob, I notice we're a little bit behind on this prescribed schedule, and and I have been reminded by the front office of our commitment to meet that schedule for the laboratory. Are there any particular reasons that explain our problems that I don't understand, and are there any things that I could help you with to move us back on a prescribed course?" This latter communication is problem oriented, describes the problem, and does not assume the superior-controlling tone of the first approach. The probability of positive results with this latter approach is considerably higher, and the subordinate will spend less time defending against a personal attack on his or her status.

The Five C's of Effective Communication

In a recent book entitled *The New Management,* Robert M. Fulmer provides a checklist for refining a spoken or written communication which he refers to as "the five C's of communication."[12] Fulmer maintains that if a message rates high in each of the five categories, it is likely to be successful in transplanting ideas from one individual to another. The important elements of this checklist are as follows.

1. *Clarity:* A communicative message needs to be straightforward and logically stated. An important point to keep in mind is that virtually three-fourths of the words in the English language have more than one meaning.

2. *Completeness:* It is important that all the essential elements of a message be contained in the communication. Sometimes only part of a message leads to misunderstanding and serious difficulties.

3. *Conciseness:* Most employees and managers alike are busy people, and to read page after page or listen for a long period of time to a manager communicate matters increases the probability of misunderstanding, lack of

listening, or distortion in the message itself. Managers should practice condensing what they say in a concise and complete manner.

4. *Concreteness:* Communication is more effective if it is based on fact, which is clearly delineated in specific terms.

5. *Correctness:* Many times employees are quick to understand and learn when communications are incorrect or inaccurate. And it is important for the manager, in building a successful image as a leader, to have a reputation for telling the truth to subordinates.

An understanding and application of these five C's of communication can be very helpful to the manager of engineering and scientific personnel.

How to Improve One-to-One and One-to-Group Communications*

There are several pointers that can be helpful to the technical manager who desires to improve the level of communications within his or her organization. These are outlined below:

1. All communication is much more effective if it is not simply a blanket communication. For instance, a communication such as, "Sue, I want you to do this," is much more effective than a general announcement at a meeting that a certain task must be accomplished by the group or some individual within the group. In the former instance, the communication is directed toward both a person and a purpose, but in the latter instance it is not.

2. It is important to understand that subordinates may not tell management how they really feel, which is commonly referred to as *filtering.* Subordinates filter because they believe that bad or realistic news may be used against them later on by the management. A good manager does not use negative information against cooperative employees.

3. Good managers should not stress to employees that their information is vitally important and will be considered very carefully. Stressing the importance of messages is often perceived by subordinates to mean that what they say is likely to be used against them if it is negative or critical, and they will filter their information carefully.

4. Every communication deserves a response; when a question is asked, a specific statement is made that is indicative of an appropriate response,

---

*The authors are indebted to Professor Hank Karp of Old Dominion University for some of the material contained in this section.

and a reply should be given, even if that reply is "no." Subordinates are often very quickly turned off when managers do not take action on their problems. The technical manager should pay attention to subordinates and make them feel that they are a significant part of the organization by both responding to and hopefully taking action on reasonable requests.

5. Abrupt interruption or change of subject during a conversation makes a subordinate feel insignificant. Good communicators bring action or closure on initiated messages from subordinates before other matters are discussed or interruptions become too distracting. Since a manager is judged by his or her subordinates through action more than words, the effectiveness of communication is reduced when managerial promises are not fulfilled. Every manager should be careful about making "empty promises" to temporarily alleviate employee conflict.

6. It is recognized that due to advanced training, scientific and engineering personnel may use complex and technical language in communicating their ideas and problems to managers and others. This fact may result in communication breakdowns between engineers and other nontechnical employee groups, which can impede managerial effectiveness. Good managers often encourage engineering and scientific personnel to use more common and understandable words in dealing with others as a means of alleviating this problem.

7. It is useful to avoid talking about things in history when responding verbally to specific subordinates. Remember, it is the present or future and not the past that is perceived as being most important, and often the relationship between these is not understood or appreciated by the subordinates.

8. The engineering manager should avoid saying "yes but" when he or she means "no," because wrong interpretations can lead to much greater problems later on. Often a manager's desire to be liked leads to a "yes but" when "no" is meant; however, the end result may be less respect and friendship from subordinates than an honest "no" will provide.

9. Managers should minimize the number of levels through which a message passes because more levels increase distortion, which is a frequent cause of communication breakdown. Drucker argues that the multiplication of the number of management levels is the most common and serious symptom of malorganization.[13] Each technical manager should strive to minimize the number of management levels for the shortest possible chain of command.

10. It is important not to overload a message with more information than can be comprehended by the receiver which results in communication breakdown.

11. Studies show that a combination of oral and written communication is most effective.[14] Thus, vitally important information to subordinates should be communicated both orally and in writing.

12. Technical managers should focus more on the purpose and direction of communication and tailor it to specific work needs rather than focus on the volume of information flow. A recent study involving the engineering and scientific environment concludes that the direction and amount of communication to other organizational units is more important then the overall amount of communication.[15] Results of this same study suggest that more successful project managers tailor their communication patterns to fit their specific work needs.

Summary

This chapter has contained a concise analysis of the realities and complexities involved in attaining effective communication in the engineering and scientific environment. Given the primary importance of communication, much attention has been given to specific action that technical managers can take to improve their communication skills. The development of good organizational communication is the cornerstone of building a results-oriented engineering or research team. Technical managers who maintain effective communication and develop teamwork among their subordinates will have taken the basic steps that are necessary to prove to top management that they are very capable managers.

Notes

1. J. Czepiel, Patterns of Inter-Organizational Communication and the Diffusion of a Major Technological Innovation. *Academy of Management Journal*, vol. 18, no. 1, 1975, pp. 6-14.

2. P. Diehl and J. R. Howell, Improving Communication within the R & D Team. *Research Management*, vol. XIX, no. 1, January 1976, pp. 23-27.

3. Marian B. McLeod, The Communication Problems of Scientists in Business and Industry. *Journal of Business Communication*, vol. 15, no. 3, Spring 1978, pp. 27-35.

4. Keith Davis, The Care and Cultivation of the Corporate Grapevine. *Dun's Review*, July 1973, pp. 44-47.

5. Keith Davis, Grapevine Communication among Lower and Middle Managers. *Personnel Journal*, April 1969, pp. 269-272.

6. *Ibid.*

7. Merwyn A. Hayes, Nonverbal Communication Without Words, in *Readings in Interpersonal and Organizational Communication* (Huseman, Logue, and Freshley, eds.), Holbrook Press, Boston, 1977, pp. 55-68.

8. Peter F. Drucker, *Management: Tasks Responsibilities,* Harper & Row, New York, 1973, p. 548.

9. Joseph Luft, *Group Processes: An Introduction to Group Dynamics,* National Press, Palo Alto, Calif., 1963.

10. Thomas J. Allen, Communications in the Research and Development Laboratory. *Technology Review,* vol. 70, no. 1, October-November 1967, pp. 31-37.

11. Jack R. Gibb, Defensive Communication. *Journal of Communication,* vol. XI, no. 3, September 1961, pp. 141-148.

12. Robert M. Fulmer, *The New Management,* Macmillan, New York, 1978, pp. 278-280.

13. Drucker, *Management,* p. 548.

14. D. A. Level, Communication Effectiveness: Method and Situation. *Journal of Business Communication,* Fall 1972, pp. 19-25.

15. Michael L. Tushman, Technical Communication in R & D Laboratories: The Impact of Project Work Characteristics. *Academy of Management Journal,* vol. 21, no. 4, December 1978, pp. 624-645.

8

Motivating the Technical Employee

Technical Managers Must Motivate Their Subordinates

Motivation of employees continues to be a major problem for almost all types of managers. While managers of creative scientists and engineers often have the advantage of highly self-disciplined subordinates, they may still experience motivational problems because of the complex needs of these employees.[1] Responses to questionnaires by industrial engineers and scientists have indicated that, as a group, over 50 percent of them believe that their needs are different from those of other workers.[2] One study of research and development personnel indicated that over two-thirds of the sample had common personality traits significantly different from the normal population. Specifically, the typical technical employee is a high achiever, nonconforming, low in guilt feelings, and has lower needs for others.[3]

While an understanding of much of the rich body of literature from applied behavioral science can be very helpful to technical managers in raising performance levels, this knowledge must be specifically adapted to the engineering and scientific environment. This chapter will adapt modern knowledge of motivation to the technical manager's needs and provide insight into the use of the motivational tools and techniques which are helpful to these managers in improving performance. George Bucher and Richard Gray, in discussing the engineering supervisor's role in motivating subordinates, suggest that these managers should be strongly encouraged to learn about human relations and motivation because ignorance of this aspect of the managerial role is an invitation to failure.[4] One study of research and development managers which supports these conclusions found that those managers who received the highest performance ratings were those who considered their role as a motivator as more important than did those managers in two lower performance categories.[5] In essence, the engineering manager's concern for motivation among subordinates impacts positively on performance, but several managers in this study expressed little interest in the motivational problem.

In order to be effective managers, engineering and scientific supervisors should confront the issue of employee motivation directly, and be well versed in the modern tools and techniques that can provide substantial help in making that confrontation successful. In spite of what many management practitioners believe, there is considerable agreement among leading behavioral scientists on what it takes to motivate the modern employee. As developed in Chapter 6, employees exhibit clear-cut needs that are emergent over a long period of development from infancy to adulthood. Behavioral research has been able to demonstrate clearly that employees are motivated directly by management's ability to link job performance to the satisfaction of these emergent needs. At the outset, two problems often face engineering and scientific managers in accomplishing this task. First, as previously pointed out, studies show that these needs are often both different and more complex for engineers and scientists than for many other occupational groups. Second, managerial restrictions and controls from outside organizations, such as Civil Service and labor unions, or simply the inability of the engineering manager to focus on these complex and different needs can cause motivation to break down or be nonexistent in many situations.

Six important steps or elements of the employee motivation process will now be developed. While it is not argued that these steps provide all the answers to difficult and complex motivational problems, a knowledge of each step will be extremely helpful to today's technical manager. Although these steps apply to many organizational environments, each step will be specifically analyzed in the engineering and scientific context. The primary emphasis will be on practical application rather than theoretical development, and several research studies will be used to document many of the significant conclusions. Simply stated, the six steps to successful employee motivation are as follows:

Proper understanding of the managerial function

Attaining mutual agreement on job expectations with subordinates

Understanding the relationship between employee selection and motivation

Developing the ability to apply popular and useful motivation models

Realizing the complex impact of money on motivation

Learning how to deal with ineffective performers

Understanding the Managerial Function

The first basic step involved in motivating any employee is to understand the managerial function. Specifically, it is the function of the manager to manage the work for the employee and not to actually do the employee's job. The managerial function is essentially a facilitative function which involves planning, organizing, and providing the support needed so that subordinates can carry out assigned tasks effectively and efficiently. All too many managers fail to delegate, or if they do delegate, they continue to try to perform the work for the subordinate. This kind of activity consumes managerial time and energy that is being devoted to the wrong thing. Energy that should be used to strengthen the planning, organization, and facilitative functions that are so important to sound management practice instead is ultimately interfering with the ability of the subordinates to do the job. Because of their innovative and self-disciplined nature, engineers and scientists are very likely to respond negatively to managerial interference. Engineering managers are usually promoted into management from technical functions that they supervise. While this technical knowledge is useful and necessary, particularly at the lower echelons of management, these managers must learn when and where not to apply it. There is a natural tendency for those managers, whose educational training and experience is similar to their subordinates, to be reluctant to delegate important job tasks and to continue to perform these duties as managers. A strong conscious effort to learn when and how to delegate is important to effective technical management, because failure to delegate is often regarded as managerial interference by subordinates. In other words, job duties important to subordinate development and satisfaction are being interfered with and largely performed by supervisors. Managerial action of this type is a major factor that reduces the sense of responsibility associated with job performance. In a survey of 282 employees of Texas Instruments, Inc., which included several engineers and scientists, Myers found that lack of responsibility was the most detrimental long-term factor that created dissatisfaction within these two employee groups.[6]

Since there are only so many hours devoted to work activities in any given time period, managers who perform subordinate tasks are taking critical time away from their planning and organizational activities. Inadequate attention devoted to planning, organizational, and facilitative functions can substantially reduce levels of potential employee motivation.

In conclusion, technical supervisors need to understand the full impact of the managerial function on the development and motivation of subordinates. While more insight into this matter is contained in Chapter 9 on leadership, four important points are as follows:

1. All developmental activities that are within the province of the employees' work should be delegated.

2. Avoid performing tasks as a manager that reduce subordinate responsibility.

3. Before performing tasks that are clearly nonmanagerial, be sure to determine if subordinates could not perform these same tasks satisfactorily. If

they can, managerial time can probably be spent more valuably on other duties, namely, planning, organizing, and facilitating.

4. Be sensitive to cues from subordinates that suggest unwarranted interference with their work.

Attainment of Mutual Agreement on Job Expectations

The second step in motivation involves managerial discussion with the subordinate that is designed to reach agreement over job expectations for a given period of time, namely, to gain an understanding with the employee on what can be accomplished. This is commonly referred to as *mutual goal setting,* which is an important part of the currently popular tool, management by objectives, which will be discussed in detail in Chapter 11. Reaching agreement with subordinates on duties and responsibilities minimizes interpersonal conflict on sensitive areas between superiors and subordinates, and increases commitment to task through personal interaction. Several studies emphasize the importance of feedback to both good communication and motivation in the engineering and scientific environment.[7] Agreement on job duties also helps to keep the subordinates focused on the more important objectives for the departmental unit; without it, subordinates may concentrate on work activities that are given a low priority by their manager.

Importance of the Facilitative Managerial Role

Once agreement has been reached on an expected level of accomplishment for the subordinate, discussion can then turn to the type of managerial support needed to attain these specific objectives. For example, sometimes a manager can make transportation available for sales calls to clients, provide secretarial help, maintenance, or other types of assistance. All of these things help the manager to be perceived as supportive, which the research continues to show is given very high marks by subordinates. It is particularly important that the supervisor be willing to go to bat for subordinates and to take interest in their problems. Subordinates should feel that it is useful to sit down and talk with superiors about their problems. Research conducted at the University of Michigan shows that these kinds of supervisory practices often determine whether employee and work group attitudes will be favorable or unfavorable.[8]

In view of these facts, it is important for each manager to answer the following question: *Am I managing properly?* Specifically:

Am I planning work activities so that it is easier for my subordinates to accomplish their assigned tasks;

Have I helped them organize their work?

Have I organized their relationships in the office, laboratory, or plant so that they have easy access to people or equipment that can help them?

Can they understand how their work relates to the total end product or end result desired?

Do I have frequent control mechanisms set up that enable me to determine when their progress is straying off course, so that I can assist them to recover before serious damage occurs, which may result in reprimanding or other negative communication?

Am I taking an interest in my subordinates as people and not simply treating them as instruments of production?

The more these questions are given an affirmative answer by the technical manager, the greater the probability exists that his or her work group will have favorable work attitudes that are likely to result in high levels of sustained motivation. Any of these questions that have a negative response suggest areas where changes in supervisory practices and behavior should increase effectiveness.

Relationship Between Employee Selection and Motivation

The third important step involved in motivating subordinates is to clearly understand the role of selection and placement in the motivational process. Many behavioral scientists recognize the fact that the quality of the employee often determines his or her level of motivation. There is considerable evidence that employees with high growth needs are motivated by interesting and challenging jobs, but employees with low growth needs are extremely difficult or impossible to motivate.[9] As discussed in Chapter 6, an employee who has very high intelligence and an extremely mature personality is not going to respond well to a job that is very immature and has little challenge or intrinsic satisfaction associated with its performance. On the other hand, an employee who has immature need development, which relates to lower intelligence and less education, may respond satisfactorily to a simple job and regard it as challenging, but some of these employees are not motivated with any job assignment. Technical managers should analyze the relative maturity and intrinsic satisfaction contained in the jobs that they are managing, because this is a necessary step in matching the intrinsic nature of these jobs with appropriate individuals whose level of maturity would suggest that the job would be satisfying to their own personality needs.

A strong argument has been made for taking the simple jobs and making them more satisfying and challenging to mature employees because these workers are more flexible and will contribute better quality performance to the organization. This process is commonly referred to as *job enrichment,* and many studies indicate that job enrichment increases the motivational level of mature employees.[10]

The good technical managers are, in part, miniature personnel managers who understand managerial functions and the problem of selecting employees whose needs match the job for which they are responsible.

Popular and Useful Motivation Models

As a fourth step in the motivation process, it is desirable to be able to apply the most useful elements of the most practical motivation models. Several behavioral scientists have made substantial contributions toward understanding human motivation during the last quarter century. Four of the most useful motivation models that have current widespread applicability to the technical environment are Abraham Maslow's Hierarchy of Needs, Douglas McGregor's Theory X and Theory Y, Frederick Herzberg's Motivation Hygiene Theory, and Victor Vroom's Expectancy Theory of Motivation.[11] A recent study of 300 practicing personnel managers in the United States indicates that the content of McGregor's approach is familiar to approximately 9 out of 10 of the managers surveyed.[12] Herzberg's Motivation Hygiene Theory ranks a close second in this same survey, and Maslow's Hierarchy of Needs ranks a respectable third. Eighty-seven percent of the managers surveyed are familiar with Herzberg's work, and eighty-three percent are familiar with the work of Maslow. Thus, three of the four motivation models are very widely known, and the Vroom model is becoming increasingly familiar to practicing managers.

Maslow's Hierarchy of Needs

Since the Maslow model is a good categorization of the specific needs of individuals, it has already been mentioned in the section of Chapter 6 that dealt with individual need development. This same model also provides an excellent beginning to the understanding of other popular motivation models because it introduces an assumption about motivation which is agreed to by most behavioral scientists. This assumption simply stated is that all behavior is a function of needs satisfaction, namely, employees are motivated to the extent that they perceive that performance of a given act will relate to the satisfaction of a specific need. Moreover, Maslow indicates that satisfied needs do not motivate. Basic physiological and safety needs which make up the lower part of the Maslow hierarchy are the strongest potential motivators. Since almost all current engineering and scientific work environments satisfy these needs, the upper level needs which include ego, self-esteem, and status offer the greatest motivational potential.[13]

Several elements of the Maslow Hierarchy of Needs model have been subjected to empirical testing with mixed results. While some components relate to increased effectiveness under given sets of conditions, other elements have been suspect. Nevertheless, Maslow's approach does show that the upper level needs of engineers and scientists are motivators in many organizational environments, and managers who take steps to satisfy these needs by initiating both environmental change and altering management style can improve management performance.

McGregor's Theory X and Theory Y

An understanding of Douglas M. McGregor's Theory X and Theory Y is helpful in providing direction to the proper modification of management style and organizational environment. This approach places considerable emphasis on the organizational environment as a primary factor in determining levels of motivation.[14] McGregor's argument is that practicing managers have traditionally been very reluctant to allow workers any amount of freedom in performing their jobs because they believe that workers are inherently lazy and will take advantage of management by doing little work unless they are closely supervised or policed while on the job. McGregor identifies this conventional approach to management as Theory X. He maintains that Theory X management stifles creativity, but instead of increasing output and motivation, it actually reduces effectiveness because it is human nature to resist this type of control. The application of Theory X insults the worker's intelligence, which McGregor believes is greater than managers are willing to accept. In contrast, McGregor proposes that management create a freer environment that enables workers to fully utilize their intrinsic abilities. This new environment trusts the worker's willingness to work, thereby minimizing the need for close supervision, and creates jobs that are more challenging and interesting because it provides for greater amounts of worker responsibility.

While McGregor's conclusions can be questioned in some organizational situations, they seem to have particular applicability to the technical environment. Several studies have already been cited which indicate that engineers and scientists prefer large amounts of autonomy and work best in an environment that is conducive to responsibility, growth, and recognition. This is precisely the type of environment that McGregor proposes in Theory Y. Many modern organizations characterize themselves as managing by a Theory Y philosophy, and there is considerable evidence to encourage this approach in the engineering and scientific work environment.

The Great Jackass Fallacy

Additional support for McGregor's and Maslow's work is provided by Harry Levinson in a recent analysis of the motivational problem.[15] Levinson concludes that in spite of all that has been written about motivation in recent years, managers continue to rely heavily on two primary means to motivate employees, namely, the carrot and stick. The carrot provides the reward, but if this fails, the stick is used to punish individuals that exhibit uncooperative behavior. This approach is similar to what has been traditionally applied to motivate a "jackass," and the employee is, consequently, being managed in much the same fashion. While the "jackass" is often resistant and does not respond to these techniques, the human employee is likely to present an even greater problem.

Since employees are more intelligent than jackasses, they not only fail to respond to these two motivational techniques, but often outsmart the management. As Levinson points out, they figure out ways to get the carrot and avoid the stick. Since the carrot is primarily measured in dollars, management continues to pay more money for less performance. For example, common job security provisions in collective bargaining agreements and Civil Service regulations make it extremely difficult for employers to discharge poorly motivated employees or even to use milder forms of disciplinary action. On the other hand, these same bargaining agreements historically have provided substantial wage and fringe benefit packages that apply to all employees covered in the contract.

Due to competitive pressure, precedent, and because it often breeds less conflict, managers in technical environments are likely to distribute rewards on an even basis among subordinates. These same pressures, coupled with a strong sense of professionalism, may make managers reluctant to punish problem performers. The end result is that these employees who do less are often protected from the stick, but are still able to get their average share of the carrot. Consequently, there is a logical argument that strongly suggests the carrot and stick approaches to motivation are often not effective. These two traditional motivational techniques are important elements of conventional management as described in McGregor's Theory X.

Levinson argues that a better approach to motivation focuses on employee needs and stresses the fact that effective managers should attempt to understand the need structure of their employees. The organizational environment should be supportive of those needs for motivation to take place.

Motivation Hygiene Theory

Frederick Herzberg developed his Motivation Hygiene Theory in the mid 1950s, and this approach has gained a considerable following and some empirical testing over the last 20 years. Herzberg maintained that the work environment could be divided into two sets of factors as follows: First, factors that lead to employee growth and development; namely, recognition, advancement, achievement, and the job itself, which he defined as motivators. Second, according to Herzberg, the environment also contains hygiene factors such as wages, working conditions, company policy, and supervision, which essentially maintain the work place for the employee.[16] One of the basic elements in the Herzberg approach is that hygiene factors affect job dissatisfaction and improving hygiene reduces dissatisfaction for a given employee. In contrast, motivators affect job satisfaction, and employee motivation is a function of the level of job satisfaction. Herzberg maintains that job satisfaction and job dissatisfaction are two mutually exclusive factors in the organizational environment.[17] A central point in his approach to motivation is that motivation is not increased by manipulating the hygiene factors, but can only be improved through the application and development of motivational factors. This process, as indicated earlier in this chapter, is known as job enrichment, which has been shown to impact favorably on motivation. From 1954 to 1958, Herzberg and his associates at the Psychological Service of Pittsburgh interviewed approximately 200 engineering and accounting personnel employed in industrial firms in the Pittsburgh area in order to gain insight into the relationship between job attitudes and performance. Each respondent was asked to discuss a time when he felt exceptionally good or exceptionally bad about his job, and to identify the factor(s) most responsible for those feelings. The five most commonly mentioned causes of dissatisfaction (bad feeling) were company policy, technical supervision, salary, supervisory relationships, and working conditions. The five satisfiers (good feeling) mentioned most frequently were achievement, recognition, the work itself, responsibility, and advancement.[18] Since the differences between engineers and accountants were negligible with regard to dissatisfiers and only moderately significant among the satisfiers, these findings are useful to managers of technical employees.[19] They specifically support the fact that Herzberg's factors that contribute to motivation and dissatisfaction are applicable to the engineering work environment.

Keith Davis conducted a similar study of 36 engineers in a Phoenix electronics firm.[20] Each engineer was asked through a questionnaire to report in detail a situation resulting in strongly favorable feelings toward the job and another situation resulting in unfavorable feelings about the job. The results of this study are reported in Table 8.1. These data generally support Herzberg's findings. The same factors show up as motivators (satisfiers) and hygiene (dissatisfiers) as in previous studies, including Herzberg's. This table also indicates the neutrality of salary, which is consistent with other research data. A dozen studies involving 1685 employees in a variety of occupations found salary to rank only slightly higher as a hygiene factor than as a motivator.[21] Apparently, wages can be either a motivator or hygiene factor which places them in a unique category. The special role of remuneration in motivation will be given special attention later in this chapter.

Achievement was the most frequently identified motivator, which is consistent with Myers' survey of engineers and scientists at Texas Instruments, Inc.[22] As can be seen in Table 8.1, recognition and advancement ranked high as a motivator among engineers surveyed. Incidentally, Myers found that recognition is a relatively stronger motivator for scientists than for engineers at Texas Instruments, but advancement provided stronger incentive for engineers than scientists.

Table 8.1 Percentage of Job Factors Appearing in Favorable and Unfavorable Job Incidents as Reported by 36 Engineers

Job factor	% Favorable[a]	% Unfavorable[a]
Motivational factors (ranked in order of favorable appearance)		
Achievement	55	8
Recognition	33	8
Advancement	22	3
Work itself	19	11
Possibility of growth	14	8
Responsibility	14	3
Maintenance factors (ranked in order of unfavorable appearance)		
Company policy and administration	5	44
Supervision–technical	8	22
Interpersonal relations– supervisor	5	19
Salary	11	11
Interpersonal relations–peers	0	8
Job security	0	8
Personal life	0	5
Working conditions	0	5
Interpersonal relations– subordinates	0	0
Status	0	0

[a]The percentages for each column total more than 100 percent because more than one factor could appear in a single incident.

Source: From Keith Davis, "How Do You Motivate Your Engineers and Scientists?" *Arizona Business Bulletin,* Bureau of Business and Economic Research, Arizona State University, Tempe, Ariz., February 1969, pp. 27-32.

In a study designed to identify important features of an engineer's or a scientist's work relating to productivity, Vincent and Mirakhor found that a statistically significant relationship existed between productivity and job satisfaction.[23] Overall, management activities that increase job satisfaction will impact favorably on motivation.

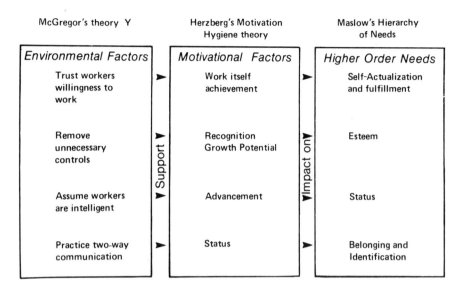

Figure 8.1   Basic similarities among McGregor's Theory Y, Herzberg's Motivation Hygiene Theory, and Maslow's Hierarchy of Needs

It should now be clear that knowledge of the Herzberg approach to motivation is particularly important to technical managers because empirical evidence indicates that it is directly applicable. Managerial attention to providing an engineering and scientific work environment in which achievement, recognition, and advancement flourish can substantially raise performance levels. Supervisors who take a special interest in the design of jobs and can provide tasks that are both challenging and rewarding should also attain high payoffs.

Similarities and Differences Among the Approaches of Maslow, McGregor, and Herzberg

Figure 8.1 shows some of the important similarities among the Maslow model, McGregor's approach, and Herzberg's Motivation Hygiene Theory. All three models emphasize the growth needs of individuals and imply that a democratic style of management will be effective in raising the level of employee performance. As can be seen in Figure 8.1, an integrated relationship exists among these three approaches to motivation. Maslow focuses on the identification and development of individual needs, Herzberg puts these needs in the context of the job and supervision, and McGregor stresses the importance of the total organizational environment. Each approach supports the other; McGregor's environmental factors foster the development of Herzberg's motivational factors, which in turn relate to the satisfaction of higher level needs.

There are also important differences in these three approaches. For example, while Maslow assumes that any need can be a motivator if it is relatively unsatisfied, Herzberg argues that only higher needs serve as motivators, and that a worker can be relatively dissatisfied in both higher order and lower order need areas simultaneously. Maslow's lower order need areas are similar to Herzberg's hygiene factors.

The level of dissatisfaction can become so great that motivational factors are meaningless. For example, although wages may be considered a special case, if the average annual compensation for a specific type of engineer in a given geographical location is in excess of $50,000, an engineer in this area with similar training and experience that receives only $30,000 annually might not respond to motivational factors. The lower rate of pay received relative to other engineers would result in so much dissatisfaction that job enrichment activities would be useless. Similarly, company policy or working conditions may be so poor that employees do not respond to either recognition or interesting task assignments.

While all empirical testing of Herzberg's model does not prove its validity in all situations, as previously indicated, research suggests that it is particularly useful in solving some of the motivational problems commonly associated with managing engineers, scientists, and professional staff. It also helps to put part of the work of Maslow and McGregor in a more meaningful context. It stresses the importance of higher order needs and the environmental factors of job enrichment which are part of the McGregor's Theory Y and focuses on the specific needs in the Maslow model that have the greatest potential for motivation. Herzberg's motivational factors are particularly important to engineers and scientists. The technical manager should help provide a work environment that encourages the development and use of recognition, advancement, achievement, and growth, as well as an interesting and challenging job.

Application of the Herzberg Model

Frederick Herzberg has provided clues as to how this model can be applied, and some of his most useful points follow.[24] (1) Eliminate simple and nonchallenging job responsibilities when possible; (2) communicate directly with employees, thereby minimizing levels and distortions in the communication process; (3) delegate to subordinates a considerable degree of responsibility for their work; (4) allow and encourage employees to become specialists in their fields of interest; (5) if the employee serves a client, encourage that client relationship to become personal and rewarding; (6) reward and recognize subordinates who do outstanding work. Since many of these suggestions can be applied without additional financial or administrative support, they are valuable to all engineering and scientific managers.

There is considerable research evidence that indicates that scientists who engage in a variety of work are more productive.[25] Thus, when engineering and scientific managers encourage subordinates to be specialists in their fields of interest, they must be careful that the end result is not narrow specialization with little variety. In direct support of Herzberg, studies show that engineers and scientists have more job satisfaction when there is more challenge in their jobs.[26] A variety of interesting and challenging work assignments among subordinates will reduce the motivational problems that confront the engineering and scientific manager.

Vroom's Expectancy Theory

The Expectancy Theory of Motivation developed in detail by Victor Vroom and refined by Lawler and Porter and others is a motivational model that is receiving increasing attention by managers.[27] The model is based on the assumption that motivation is a product of the needs one seeks to fulfill and an estimate by that individual that certain acts will lead to the fulfillment of those needs. In general, expectancy is the belief that a particular act will yield a particular outcome. For example, if an engineer believes that hard work will result in highly rated performance, then a strong expectation exists regarding hard work and positive performance evaluation.

The Vroom model attempts to determine those outcomes that are pleasurable and those that are painful by including the concept of second-level outcomes.[28] The second-level outcomes are events that happen based on the course of action from the first-level outcome as shown in Figure 8.2. The method of determining preferences for first-level outcomes makes use of two terms, *valence* and *instrumentality*. The mathematical relationship of these terms follows:

$$V_j = f_j \left(\sum_{k=1}^{n} V_k I_{jk} \right) \quad j = 1, 2, \ldots, n$$

where

V_j = valence of outcome j, first level

V_k = valence of outcome k, second level

I_{jk} = perceived instrumentality of outcome j for the attainment of outcome k
$(-1 \leq I_{jk} \leq 1)$

Applying the above equation to the alternatives shown in Figure 8.2 will further explain the model. The valence of the first-level outcome 1 is

$$V_1 = f_1 \left(\sum_{k=1}^{2} V_k I_{jk} \right)$$
$$f_1 (V_1 I_{11} + V_2 I_{12})$$

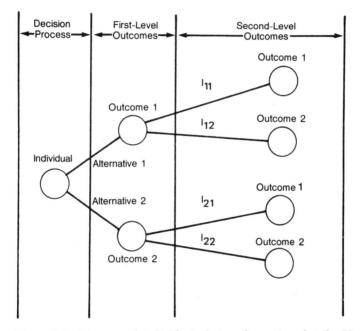

Figure 8.2 Diagram of individual choice alternatives for the Vroom model

The valence of the first-level outcome 2 is

$$V_2 = f_2 \left(V_1 I_{21} + V_2 I_{22} \right)$$

Valence refers to the strength of a person's preference for one outcome versus other possible outcomes. Those outcomes that are strongly desired, such as advancement or recognition, would have very high valences, and less preferable outcomes would have lower valences. Examples of outcomes of lower preference could include a minor change in management policy or a rearrangement of office furniture. If an individual has no preference for an outcome, the valence would then be zero; or if it were preferred that an outcome did not happen, then the valence would have a negative value.

Instrumentality indicates an individual's perception of the relationship between a first- and second-level outcome. In the previous example, if hard work and good performance are perceived to be likely to yield a promotion, there is a high degree of instrumentality present. Thus, promotion would be the second-level outcome. Expectancy differs from instrumentality in that it relates efforts to first-level outcomes, whereas instrumentality relates first- and second-level outcomes to each other. For example, if an engineer believes that he or she has the ability to be perceived as doing a good job, then that person would possess a high degree of expectancy. If good performance is perceived by this engineer as leading to a promotion, then a high degree of instrumentality would be present. If promotion is a highly valued end result, this employee is likely to be motivated to do good work.

Thus, it is clear that both instrumentality and expectancy are critical factors in determining performance behavior patterns.

Usefulness and Application of Expectancy Theory

There have been several studies by Vroom, Galbraith, Cummings, and Hill that give credibility to the Vroom model. Specifically, research supports Vroom's contention that motivation is related to productivity in those situations where the acquisition of desired goals is related to one's individual production.[29] It is clear that reinforcement is a vital factor in Vroom's approach, and it is continuously necessary for the technical manager to provide instrumentality by rewarding employees for good performance. Several authorities on motivation including Lawler stress the vital importance of relating rewards to employee performance.[30] Considering the work of Maslow, Argyris, and others, there are a variety of methods for satisfying higher level needs which are the desired outcomes that expectancy theory often is based on. In fact, there are more vehicles available to the technical manager for satisfying higher level needs than lower level needs, because these needs are never completely satisfied for normal employees.[31] Thus, the typical engineer or scientist never reaches a point of complete satisfaction with his or her accomplishments because as one set of job goals are attained, new goals which require different and often greater accomplishment take their place. Most engineering and scientific employees are capable of being continuously motivated by managers who help them realize their goals, recognize their accomplishments, and then help them set new work-related goals that will provide even greater internal satisfaction when attained.

Complex Impact of Money on Motivation

An important consideration in motivating subordinates is to understand how remuneration influences individual and group performance so that it can be placed in its proper perspective with other motivational tools. Money is often seen as the cornerstone of perceived equity in an organizational environment. If money is improperly handled by the manager, and its distribution is seen as unfair, then the perceived favorableness of the organizational environment by employees may be reduced to such a low level that other motivational factors simply do not work effectively. It is totally fallacious to assume that since engineers and scientists are highly self-disciplined, well-educated, and achievement oriented, money is of little importance to them. Money, in fact, measures many of their achievements, and because of their high degree of intelligence and education, they are quick to perceive any inequities that may exist in the remuneration process.

The proper use of wages and salaries substantially increases managerial effectiveness. Some helpful points about constructive management of the remuneration process are as follows:

1. A technical manager should retain control over some "dollar pool" for merit increases that is distributed periodically to subordinates for good performance.

2. Managers should clearly communicate to subordinates the criteria that will be used in the distribution of merit increases. It is often desirable to solicit input from subordinates in the development of these criteria.

3. Effective wage and salary administration is a continuous process, and attempts should constantly be made to have wage and salary equity within the subordinate group. Equitable wage and salary conditions usually have two fundamental characteristics: First, a direct relationship exists between perceived skill requirements and job difficulty, and pay scales; and second, both seniority and good performance are recognized with salary increments.

4. Most employees see wage reductions as seriously threatening their self-esteem, and strongly resist any action that reduces their pay. Obviously, motivation, morale, and performance can be adversely affected. When individual employees are overpaid, it is often necessary to handle these problems through natural attrition and the granting of smaller pay raises than those amounts given to other employees.

5. Although it may be corporate policy that individual wages and salaries are to be kept secret, do not assume that this secrecy can be guaranteed. In fact, if significant inequities exist they will probably surface and will have to be dealt with. Consequently, wage and salary equity is vitally important in all organizations.

6. Always consider the impact of specific salary adjustments, merit increases, or bonuses on other subordinates. The impact of these "money" decisions are not isolated to the subordinates who receive them, but usually spread throughout the entire subordinate group.

7. The demand for wage increases by employees may be symptomatic of more complex problems associated with the organizational climate. Since wages are very tangible and measurable, wage increases are often requested to compensate for other deficiencies that are less tangible and harder to verbalize. For example, subordinates may be dissatisfied with the management practices of their supervisors, but find it difficult to describe or com-

plain about it. Thus, as an alternative, they request more money. In this case, however, granting a wage increase will not solve their basic problem. In order to be most effective, technical managers should identify the real problem(s) when money requests appear to be symptomatic of other issues.

In view of the above points, it should be recognized that money is a complex element in the motivational process. Although the role of money is often played down by many behavioral scientists, it is vital to employee motivation. Money is important for several reasons. First, it often measures recognition, status, advancement, and achievement. Second, it is tangible and measurable by its recipient. And third, it is the variable that often can be easily manipulated by the management of a given organization. Since it can have a positive role in reinforcing many of the motivational elements, and since in many instances it can be manipulated by the management, it may substantially raise levels of motivation among subordinates.

Corrective Action for the Ineffective Performer

During any given period of time, some specific levels of motivation may substantially decline, creating personnel problems for the technical manager and the organization. While a decline in motivation can occur at any stage in one's career, it is often associated with advancing age and tenure on the job. One study of 2500 engineers in seven large organizations found a negative correlation after age 35 between age and performance rating.[32] Specifically, engineers over 35 are more likely to receive lower performance ratings by their superiors. It is clearly not automatic that older employees will become less effective performers, because this same study found that the top third of the engineers over 50 were almost as highly valued as the top third in any age group.[33] Ineffective performers can be found in any employee age group. Engineering managers should know that although easy or total solutions to these problems do not usually exist, there are some specific managerial action steps that can be helpful. Several of the most useful steps are as follows:

1. Attempt to categorize the causes of poor performance. Causes that are related to organizational climate or management can often be corrected.

2. If the problem is psychologically based, determine if the employee will accept help. If so, make attempts to provide appropriate professional counseling. In some instances these skills are available within the organizational unit; however, it may be both necessary and worthwhile to go outside the engineering unit or company to obtain the best professional aid.

3. Recognize the importance of a dual promotional system in motivating older employees. Many engineers become dismayed when they find that

they must become managers to receive continued advancement and recognition in their firm.

4. If the employee is simply not responding to existing motivational factors, look for new and different ones that may be used.

5. If the causes of poor performance are unrelated to or beyond the control of management, the alternatives of transfer, early retirement, or discharge should be considered. Older employees who are ineffective can sometimes be given financial inducements to retire, which are less costly than inefficiencies resulting from retaining them. Younger employees that hold strategic positions where their poor performance disrupts the work of colleagues may be transferred or discharged. Specific reasons for transfer or discharge should be well documented by the manager.

6. Large numbers of ineffective performers often suggest poor placement policies or the need for better training and work orientation programs. If managerial analysis suggests that either of these conditions is causative, corrective action should be taken promptly.

7. Correcting these kinds of performance problems requires a considerable amount of managerial time, insight, and often courage. However, the ability to deal directly with the problem of ineffective performance is an important characteristic of an outstanding manager.

Building the Proper Motivational Environment

Managers in technical environments can benefit from the motivation models discussed in this chapter. Managerial attention should be given to the higher level needs of professional employees. Engineers have high needs for autonomy and freedom in their environment, and they seek recognition for achievement often in the form of increased status and advancement. Managerial practices have a lot to do with how well these needs are perceived as being met. Anything the manager can do to relieve restrictions, make the work environment more autonomous, and at the same time provide some semblance of effective control over output is an essential part of being effective. Unfortunately, there is considerable evidence that many engineering managers are failing to accomplish these managerial tasks. A poll and in-depth interview conducted a number of years ago by the Opinion Research Corporation on job satisfaction among industrial scientists and engineers revealed that only 34 percent were well satisfied.[34] In this same study, a survey of a subsample of engineers and scientists who were considered the most valuable by company management found that only 42 percent were well satisfied with their jobs. Thus, a majority felt that they were misunderstood and had little input to management. Managers were not perceived as doing an effective job, even by their most valued engineers and scientists. Moreover, there is little evidence that these attitudes are improving as rapidly as needed. A more recent study of several hundred engineers and scientists who had left their previous jobs showed that the single most important reason for leaving was the ab-

sence of motivational factors.[35] Insufficient use of acquired skills and lack of opportunity for advancement were specific factors cited as causing turnover among
these professionals. It has been emphasized throughout this chapter that these
factors are motivational in nature. Freedom and autonomy within the organizational environment permit subordinates to utilize their acquired skills, but some
control is needed to move the organization toward its goals. Pelz and Andrews
suggest that both freedom and coordination are compatible and desirable for engineers and scientists.[36] Generally, they support the conclusions of Rensis Likert
of the University of Michigan that employees in higher producing departments
believe that they exert considerable influence on decisions that affect them.

Management by objectives is an effective tool for accomplishing the difficult
but important managerial task of providing an environment characterized by
freedom, coordination, and control (see Chapter 11). One survey of problems in
scientific and engineering supervision revealed that two major difficulties were
insufficient definition of company objectives by top management and the related inability of lower level personnel to define problems.[37] Whenever possible,
mutual goal setting should take place and rewards should be related to performance based on an effective periodic review. It is not uncommon for technical
managers to be perceived by their subordinates as being bureaucratic pencil-and-
paper managers who set up obstacles to the accomplishment of important work.
Conversely, these managers see the subordinate as being a specialist who lacks
concern for efficiency or is not cost conscious. Management by objectives provides a framework for effectively addressing these problems.

Quality Circles

Another more recent tool, which has been shown in several firms to have a
favorable impact on organizational climate, is *Quality Circles*. A Quality Circle
is a specific name given to a small group (approximately 8-10 members) who do
similar work and agree to meet on a regular voluntary basis to discuss their work
quality problems. These groups analyze the causes of work related problems
and recommend solutions to their management. Also, in areas within their
purview, they take action to implement their recommended solutions.

While Quality Circles were introduced in Japan in the early 1960s, they have
only recently received significant attention by American management. These
groups are based upon the philosophy that organizational climate is a critical
element in motivation and in the quality of work life. Employees are recognized
as capable contributing members of the organization. Quality Circle members
are usually nonmanagers who share the same kinds of work, and consequently
can interact meaningfully and confront the problems associated with performing
their common tasks.

Each circle member is taught the elementary quality control techniques.
There is also a circle leader who is usually the immediate supervisor of the circle
members, and the success of the group is directly affected by his or her effective-

ness. In addition to the immediate circle leader there is a facilitator who is responsible for the overall leadership of the circle program. The facilitator is responsible for training the members and leaders, and also forms a link between each circle and the rest of the organization. These groups work within the existing organizatioal structure and are not designed to compete for power with the traditional hierarchy.

Engineering and scientific managers should be especially aware of the potential contribution Quality Circles can make to the technical work climate. Since lower level engineers and other technicians often have high needs for both autonomy and involvement, specific circles can identify issues and bring solutions to frustration in the environment. In fact, participation in the circle itself is a unique form of involvement. Finally, the circle concept provides an opportunity for technical managers to draw upon the skills of other nonmanagerial technical personnel.

Summary

It should now be clear that a specific managerial climate is optimal for motivational purposes. Some of the most useful characteristics of that climate are high trust, open communication, mutual goal setting, and economic reward that is equitable and based in large part on goal attainment. This desired climate is closely related to Rensis Likert's System IV.[38] Technical managers who recognize the importance of climate and take steps to develop it are dealing in a constructive manner with current or potential problems involving morale, motivation, and performance.

The analysis of motivation contained in this chapter, which has ranged from undertanding the managerial function to applying the more useful elements of current models, clearly suggests that motivation is not simply an application of the golden rule. Also, it is not solely a function of the personality of the people involved, and therefore unrelated to specific skills that can be learned and acquired by the manager. If technical managers go through the steps outlined in this chapter and make a sincere attempt to understand the current state-of-the-art knowledge concerning the motivational process, they can substantially improve performance within their units and make their jobs as managers much more enjoyable and rewarding. In essence, part of the intrinsic job satisfaction that Herzberg talks about in his theory that is so important to motivation can be greatly enhanced for the manager who makes a strong effort to understand the complexity of the motivational process and to apply the useful knowledge that has been developed regarding this intricate but important problem.

Notes

1. Donald C. Pelz and Frank M. Andrews, *Scientists in Organizations*, University of Michigan Institute for Social Research, Ann Arbor, Mich. 1976, p. 7.

2. Lee E. Danielson, *Characteristics of Engineers and Scientists Significant for Their Motivation*, University of Michigan Press, Ann Arbor, Mich., 1960.

3. Rex Hunt, Ira G. Salisbury, and George Whittington, Personality and R. & D. Performance. *Research/Development,* February 1965, pp. 36-40.

4. George C. Bucher and Richard C. Gray, Principles of Motivation and How to Apply Them. *Research Management,* vol. XIV, no. 3, May 1971, pp. 15-22.

5. J. A. Steger, G. Manners, A. J. Bernstein, and R. May, The Three Dimensions of the R. & D. Managers Job. *Research Management,* vol. XVIII, no. 3, May 1975, pp. 32-37.

6. M. Scott Myers, Who Are Your Motivated Workers? *Harvard Business Review,* January-February 1964, pp. 73-88.

7. P. Diehl and J. R. Howell, Improving Communication Within the Research and Development Team. *Research Management,* vol. XIX, no. 1, January 1976, pp. 23-27.

8. Rensis Likert, *New Patterns of Management,* McGraw-Hill, New York, 1961, p. 17.

9. J. Richard Hackman, Greg Oldham, Robert Janson, and Kenneth Purdy, A New Strategy for Job Enrichment, *California Management Review,* vol. XVII, no. 4, 1975.

10. *Ibid.* For additional support of the job enrichment concept, see W. J. Paul, Jr., K. B. Robertson, and F. Herzberg, Job Enrichment Pays Off. *Harvard Business Review,* 1969, pp. 61-78.

11. For a current theoretical discussion of these models, see Andrew D. Szilagyi, Jr. and Marc J. Wallace, Jr., *Organizational Behavior and Performance,* Goodyear Publishing, Santa Monica, Calif., 1980, pp. 99-140.

12. Desmond Martin and William Kearney, The Behavioral Sciences in Management Development Programs. *Journal of Business,* Seton Hall University, vol. 16, no. 2, May 1978, pp. 26-32.

13. Bucher and Gray, "Principles of Motivation and How to Apply Them."

14. Douglas M. McGregor, *The Human Side of Enterprise,* McGraw-Hill, New York, 1960.

15. For a detailed discussion of Levinson's analysis of the motivation problem, see Harry Levinson, *The Great Jackass Fallacy,* Harvard University Press, Cambridge, Mass., 1973.

16. For a concise discussion of the Motivation Hygiene Theory, see Frederick Herzberg, *Work and the Nature of Man,* World Publishing Co., Cleveland, 1966, Chapter 6.

17. *Ibid.,* p. 76.

18. For a discussion of this research, see F. Herzberg, B. Mausner, and B. B. Snyderman, *The Motivation To Work,* John Wiley & Sons, New York, 1959. For a more current discussion of the implications of this research, see also F. Herzberg, *The Managerial Choice: To be Efficient and To be Human,* Irwin, Homewood, Ill., 1974.

19. *Ibid.*

20. Keith Davis, How Do You Motivate Your Engineers and Scientists? *Arizona Business Bulletin,* February 1969, pp. 27-32.

21. Frederick Herzberg, One More Time: How Do You Motivate Your Employees? *Harvard Business Review,* January-February 1968, pp. 53-62.

22. Myers, "Who Are Your Motivated Workers?"

23. H. F. Vincent and Abbas Mirakhor, Relationship Between Productivity Satisfaction, Ability, Age and Salary in a Military R. & D. Organization. *IEEE Transactions on Engineering Management,* EM19-45, May 1972, pp. 45-53.

24. Frederick Herzberg, The Wise Old Turk. *Harvard Business Review,* September-October 1974, pp. 70-80.

25. Frank M. Andrews, Scientific Performance as Related to Time Spent on Technical Work, Teaching, or Administration. *Administrative Science Quarterly,* September 1964, pp. 182-193.

26. Douglas T. Hall and Edward E. Lawler III, Job Characteristics and Pressures and the Organizational Integration of Professionals. *Administrative Science Quarterly,* September 1970, pp. 271-281.

27. Edward E. Lawler and Lyman W. Porter, Antecedent Attitudes of Effective Managerial Performance. *Organizational Behavior and Human Performance,* vol. 2, 1967, pp. 122-142.

28. Victor H. Vroom, *Work and Motivation,* John Wiley & Sons, New York, 1964.

29. J. G. Hunt and J. W. Hill, The New Look in Motivation Theory for Organizational Research. *Human Organization,* vol. 28, no. 2, 1969.

30. Edward Lawler, *Motivation in Work Organizations,* Brooks/Cole Publishing, Monterey, Calif., 1973, p. 145.

31. Chris Argyris, Personal Versus Organizational Goals. *Yale Scientific,* February 1960, pp. 40-50.

32. Gene W. Dalton, Paul H. Thompson, and Raymond L. Price, The Four Stages of Professional Careers: A New Look at Performance by Professionals. *Organizational Dynamics,* Summer 1977, pp. 19-42.

33. *Ibid.*

34. Robert D. Best, The Scientist Versus the Management Mind. *Industrial Research,* October 1963, pp. 50-52.

35. Arthur Gerstenfeld and Gabriel Rosica, Why Engineers Transfer. *Business Horizons,* April 1970, pp. 43-48.

36. Pelz and Andrews, *Scientists in Organizations,* p. 32.

37. Lauren B. Hitchcock, Problems of First Line Supervisors. *Research Management,* vol. X, November 1967, pp. 385-397.

38. For a detailed discussion of Systems IV Management, see Rensis Likert, *The Human Organization,* McGraw-Hill, New York, 1967.

9　Leadership in the
Technical Environment

Importance of Leadership Style

One of the best ways that managers can increase the level of motivation among subordinates in an engineering or scientific environment is to be effective leaders. Leadership can be defined as a process of influence in which the leader is able to get the follower to stay on a prescribed path toward the attainment of specific goals that are desired by the leader. Thus, by definition the art of leadership is an important part of effective management. Because of their technical orientation, engineering managers are often preoccupied with the technical and scientific aspects of subordinate jobs, and often pay little attention to the development and application of leadership skills. This situation is particularly characteristic of technical supervisors at lower management levels. Studies have shown that this technical orientation decreases as engineering managers advance in the management hierarchy.[1] An understanding of leadership including the selection of style and attendant managerial relationships with subordinates is important at all levels of management.

Much has been written about leadership in the last 30 years, and some authors have developed as many as 15 or 20 possible leadership styles that can be used in managing employees. In analyzing leadership, four basic styles are delineated in this chapter. These styles are autocratic, bureaucratic, laissez-faire, and democratic. The major diferences among these styles can be determined by looking at the way the power source is perceived and used by the leader.

Autocratic Leadership

The autocratic leader perceives himself or herself as the source of power, and makes all the decisions in an organization in terms of being the absolute center of authority and control. A major advantage of working for the strict autocratic

117

leader is that the subordinate always knows where he or she stands with the leader, namely, the leader will both make decisions and take the responsibility for them. This fact simplifies work relationships for the subordinate because all the subordinate has to do is cooperate and carry out assignments. The obvious disadvantage is that creativity is stifled and individual development is neglected. Creative people such as engineers and scientists usually have great difficulty with a strict autocrat because they are highly self-disciplined and tend to be frustrated by control-oriented leaders.

A modification of the strict autocratic style is often referred to in the literature as the *benevolent autocratic style*. The benevolent autocrat makes all the decisions, but tends to constantly communicate to employees that decisions are being made in their interest. This style is, in part, an outgrowth of the "identity of interests" concept of management, which was prevalent prior to 1930. According to this concept, owners, managers, and employees of a business automatically have the same common interest, which is the growth and success of the firm. Consequently, the manager's choice and actions in leadership and decision-making situations will automatically be in the interest of the subordinates because managers are paid to run the business in the best and most efficient possible manner.

There are some difficulties with this approach to management. One problem that should be quite clear is that its success is predicated on the assumption that subordinates will accept the fact that the managers automatically know what is in their best interest and have the wisdom and judgment to make those kinds of supportive decisions. Professional people, such as engineers, can be highly critical of the managerial function. Since they are highly trained and skill oriented, they are not predisposed to accept the judgment of their leaders as being necessarily in the interest of their own goals or those of the organization.

The benevolent autocrat must continually rely on rewards to gain the support and cooperation of subordinates. If the organization experiences economic hardship and these rewards become less available or nonexistent, a crisis ensues. The impact of this state of affairs is likely to cause the subordinates to view with disfavor the actions and leadership control functions performed by their boss. Although benevolent autocracy, accompanied by rewards, has been shown to work quite well for short periods of time with nonprofessionals, situations where this style works best are not common to the professional engineering environment.

Some managers tend to practice the autocratic style simply because they are basically insecure in their jobs. Insecurity can cause managers to tighten up the reins of control because there is a subconscious feeling that greater competency is needed if more people are allowed to become involved in the decision-making process. When insecurity or fear of incompetence causes a manager to tighten up the reins of management and retain most of the decision-making authority, this leader is commonly referred to as an *incompetent autocrat*. This style of leadership is ineffective because most employees perceive that incompetence does exist, and lose respect for the manager. This fact holds true even if the decision outcomes are correct from the standpoint of the organization and the employees themselves.

While there is a substantial amount of research that suggests that autocratic management can be effective in increasing productivity, this research generally is associated with short-run time periods or situations characterized by a poor organizational climate.[2] Usually, important human relations factors such as morale, loyalty, feeling of warmth and support, and identification are not as positive under autocratic leadership. Thus, while short-run productivity may rise, there is a price being paid for this improvement by the human factors within the organization. The value of human assets may be decreasing as they are exploited by autocratic leaders.

Exploitation of human assets is recognized by Rensis Likert, who developed the idea that human resources valuation should be measured on the balance sheet along with other "tangible" assets. He concludes that certain leadership styles and management practices that are increasing the output of the organization in the short run, are actually reducing the value of its human resources in the long run; and this condition should show up in the value of the total assets of the organization. Likert calls his system for evaluating human assets *human resources accounting.*[3] Although several articles have appeared on human resources accounting in the last 10 years and there is some interest in it among practicing managers, it has had little practical usage.[4] The human resources accounting concept could be used in professional engineering-type organizations to show that since autocracy is practiced among technical managers as the basic leadership style for motivating their subordinates, the value of the engineering professional staff may in fact be decreasing.

Bureaucratic Leadership

The *bureaucratic* style of leadership is an approach that is used in many organizations. Bureaucratic styles of management are taken from the term bureaucracy, which is a system of management that utilizes formal rules and regulations as the power base. The bureaucratic leader sees rules and regulations as the power source for making decisions within the organization. When practicing this style, the leader goes by the book and does not get personally involved in the decision-making process. In a few limited instances, this can be an advantageous approach because there are times when it is desirable for the manager to be personally removed from an unpopular decision. Successful application of bureaucratic management in these kinds of situations involves convincing the subordinates that the application of rules cannot be avoided. The ability of technical managers to convince subordinates that nothing can be done about applying the rules is a function of several factors which include the subordinates' perception of the strengths and weaknesses of the manager, their training and professionalism, and their perception of the specific situation.

It is more difficult to convince professionals such as engineers and scientists that formal regulations must be followed than it is to convince paraprofessional subordinates who may have been taught to follow the rules from their induction into the organization. Also, if subordinates believe that there is nothing their managers can do about the rules, managerial strength may be altered, and the ability to motivate and gain the cooperation of subordinates is reduced. Much of the research tends to show that American subordinates prefer managers who are strong and have upward influence with their superiors in the organization.[5] The more these managers rely on rules and convince subordinates they can do nothing about these rules, the less they are perceived to have upward influence in the organizational hierarchy. Thus, the factors needed to sell bureaucracy as a style of management and to increase the managerial effectiveness are often working at cross-purposes with each other.

Bureaupathic Behavior

Several years ago, Victor Thompson pointed out some additional negative effects of bureaucratic leadership. According to Thompson, continued application of bureaucratic leadership can cause leaders to assume certain common characteristics which are described as *bureaupathic behavior.* "Bureaupathic" refers to an organizational environment with four basic characteristics: Petty insistance on the rights of office; ritualistic attachment to routines and procedures; excessive aloofness; and resistance to change.[6] These conditions result from the manager's attempt to adjust to rules and regulations which must be constantly applied. As a means of adjusting and retaining individuality in this environment, the rules and regulations become ends in themselves, and self-expression is realized through the application and protection of rights of office. Managers become excessively aloof because it becomes desirable to be insulated from the complaints and frustrations of subordinates. Change is resisted because the existing system becomes the most important factor in the managerial environment, and it is protected by individual managers against modification. Changing the system would involve managerial effort and readjustment, but change is usually not viewed as being constructive. Bureaupathic leadership impedes organizational effectiveness because it stifles creativity and increases employee frustration. Bureaupathic behavior is a tremendous liability to the professional environment which thrives on creativity, new thought processes, innovation, and initiative.

In conclusion, although an argument can be made that it may be desirable for managers to remove themselves personally from a decision-making situation by applying rules, the evidence clearly suggests that these situations are relatively few and that the liabilities of using bureaucratic leadership extensively in managing the engineering and scientific environment are great. Consequently, the usefulness of this particular leadership style to technical managers is very limited.

Laissez-faire Leadership

Laissez-faire leadership is a third style that is available to technical managers. The laissez-faire manager can be distinguished from other managers by the fact that a power source is not perceived or used, and this leader does not function as an effective personal force in managing subordinates. In spite of this apparent weakness, there are some advantages to laissez-faire management, particularly in creative professional environments. Since engineers and scientists are usually highly self-disciplined, they tend to do their best work with a minimum of interference, particularly if they maintain a lively interest in a variety of research problems.[7] This is precisely what laissez-faire management provides. Since there is no interference by the manager and the subordinate is completely free, a very autonomous environment exists. Laissez-faire leaders are only effective when problem-solving skills and knowledge necessary to do the job are self-contained within the subordinate group, because little or no help will come from the manager. Additionally, if extensive cooperation is needed among several engineers to accomplish the professional task, little goal setting or facilitative activity will come from the manager. Finally, these managers do a poor job of relating the productive efforts of the subordinate group to the greater organization. When a product is completed or a job is well done, this may not be communicated effectively to the rest of the organization, so little appreciation is gained from the greater organization to the subunit for completing their task. Similarly, recognition from the laissez-faire manager to subordinates for a job well done is often nonexistent. Earlier chapters on needs and motivation stressed that this kind of recognition is vital to professionals and engineers as well as other employee groups.

In summary, the conditions in which laissez-faire management can work are those where the job knowledge is self-contained within the subordinate unit; there is little need for inner dependency or cooperation to perform the task among unit members; and the subordinates are highly educated self-initiaters, with high levels of self-discipline. Also, laissez-faire management can be combined with certain types of communication feedback such as monthly reports by subordinates delineating that month's accomplishments, which is then passed on to the appropriate levels of upper management. In these kinds of conditions, laissez-faire management may actually work better than any other leadership style, and the level of motivation that results from its use may be high. Conversely, in situations where the job knowledge is not self-contained, a considerable amount of inner dependency is required, managerial recognition is needed to support specific accomplishments, and the relationship of subunit tasks to the greater organizational purpose is not clear, laissez-faire management will be ineffective.

Democratic Leadership

The fourth managerial style that is important to engineering and scientific managers is *democratic.* The democratic manager believes that power is derived from the subordinate group. This style gained impetus from the acceptance theory of authority as developed by Chester Barnard back in the late 1930s and was mentioned in Chapter 4. In his book, *The Functions of the Executive,* Barnard maintained that any manager's authority over a subordinate group was limited by the willingness of that group to accept the authority of the manager.[8] For example, if a boss tells a subordinate to do something, but the subordinate refuses, a serious management problem exists. It is doubtful that threats or physical force will change this behavior on any long-term basis, and acceptance of the manager's authority is necessary for long-term change. Many practicing managers have tended to accept this reasoning over the years, which has laid the groundwork for a strong belief in democratic management.

The work of the late Kurt Lewin in the 1940s involving small boys in experimental leadeship groups built a good case for democratic management. Lewin found that democratically managed boys who engaged in productive tasks exhibited more cooperation, less frustration, greater satisfaction with the task, and better overall performance than similar groups managed by laissez-faire or autocratic leaders.[9] Leadership style was shown to be more important than the personality of the leader in determining the behavioral patterns of the subordinates. However, much like Likert, in short-run situations, Lewin found productivity could be equally high or even greater among autocratic as opposed to democratically managed groups.

This analysis of style thus far could easily lead to the conclusion that democratic leadership is usually the most useful in an engineering and scientific environment. However, such a conclusion is far too simple and not necessarily supported by research data. While democratic leadership has been widely discussed and advocated by many management authorities since the mid 1950s, what the implementation of democratic management actually entails is still widely misunderstood. In order to help alleviate this confusion, it is important to point out several elements that are *not* characteristic of the democratic style.

It is *not* giving up control and total decision-making power to the subordinates.

It is *not* necessarily making decisions by majority vote among subordinates.

It is *not* allowing subordinates to become involved in decision making only when the outcome of these decisions is unimportant to the leader.

It is *not* a style of management that is designed to eliminate most conflict.

The above points are often erroneously associated with the democratic style. In looking more positively at the characteristic elements of good democratic management, the following statements are associated with sound democratic management.

1. There is true "mutual" involvement in the decision-making process, e.g., the manager and subordinates both make significant input into important decisions.

2. It is both appropriate and often necessary for the manager to be sure that the goals are set and understood by subordinates with regard to his or her organizational unit. These goals serve as both guides and boundaries which help to keep behavior on a prescribed course. The goal-setting process for management by objectives as described in detail in Chapter 11 is congruent with sound democratic principles. It is usually desirable but not always possible to solicit input from subordinates during the goal-setting process.

3. Applying democratic management requires the continuous development of subordinates. The democratic manager should help to provide a work climate that fosters the development of objectives, stimulates a capacity and desire by employees to become involved, and includes employees with varying levels of technical knowledge.

4. There are many situations where lack of knowledge or time constraints make democratic principles inappropriate, and in these cases they should not be used. These kinds of constraints are commonly associated with many situations in today's engineering groups.

Modern democratic management involves a climate of mutual trust, shared knowledge, and clear-cut goals when used properly; and technical managers should fully understand that attaining managerial effectiveness through applying democratic management techniques is a complex process.

It is increasingly apparent that the situation often dictates the appropriateness of the choice of a particular style, and that there are advantages to each of the four styles in specific situations. The major advantage of the autocratic style is that it is quick, simple, and assumes that the manager's job is simply to manage and make decisions. In many organizational activities, the right of the manager to manage goes without question, and autocratic leadership is most effective. Specific examples of situations that can be effectively handled autocratically are as follows: secretarial relationships, where it is usually the manager's job to set priorities and tell the secretary precisely what to do in terms of certain work activities; and maintenance supervision, where there is a breakdown in laboratory equipment and the job is to repair the equipment quickly. Also, in time of crisis where both time and direction are important, autocracy usually works best, and these conditions support its acceptance.

Specific situations can also favor either bureaucratic or laissez-faire approaches. Bureaucratic leadership can work in instances where disciplinary action must be invoked by rules or cases that are touchy ones from the standpoint of personalities, which make the application of rules and regulations desirable. Laissez-faire management can work best in laboratories where highly skilled Ph.D.'s are brought in for their unique expertise to research a problem. Once the problem is defined and the assignment made, these skilled technicians may work most effectively when left completely alone. However, in situations where the acceptance and quality of decisions are critical, and the growth and development of subordinates are a desired goal, the democratic style is more likely to be successful.

The real answer to the question of choosing the appropriate leadership style is a complex one, which is related to several environmental factors, including the power and personality of the decision maker or leader, the characteristics of the situation, and the time needed to perform the task. Figure 9.1 places autocratic and democratic decision making at opposite ends of a continuum, and suggests that most decision making occurs at different points along this continuum. As Figure 9.1 indicates, leaders may change their management style hourly, depending on the specific decision-making situation. Autocratic or democratic management should be depicted as a matter of degree rather than being absolute.

These conclusions are supported in a recent study of leadership effectiveness in project management by Thamhain and Wilemon, which analyzed the impact of leader-centered (autocratic) and team-centered (democratic) styles on managerial effectiveness.[10] A measure of this effectiveness was obtained through a rating of the superiors of 68 project managers. The overall quality of the work environment coupled with the application of an appropriate leadership style has the greatest impact on managerial effectiveness according to the results of this research.

In a good organizational climate characterized by good communication, work continuity, and career growth, democratic, team-oriented approaches were most effective. Where a poor climate existed, the more autocratic, leader-centered approaches worked best.[11] Two basic explanations of these results are offered. In a poor organizational climate, leader-centered direction provides order to the work and may reduce employee anxieties. In good organizational climates where communication flows freely and anxieties are low, employees are more responsive to team-building efforts. While overall conclusions from this study suggest that a good organizational climate conducive to team-centered leadership (democratic)

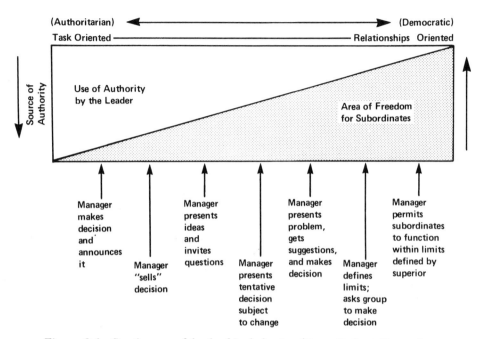

Figure 9.1 Continuum of leadership behavior (From Robert Tannenbaum and Warren H. Schmidt, "How to Choose a Leadership Pattern," *Harvard Business Review,* March-April 1958, Copyright © 1958 by the President and Fellows of Harvard College; all rights reserved.)

is preferable to a poor climate, it recognizes that technical managers need to be flexible in their approach to leadership. Flexibility is needed because the factors that determine organizational climate are beyond the control of the manager in many instances, and rapid change is not unusual in the technical work environment.

Since organizational climate is so important to managerial effectiveness, Thamhain and Wilemon offer some specific suggestions on managerial action to improve it.[12]

1. An organizational audit should take place aimed at determining the causes of poor climate.

2. A program should be undertaken to correct poor climate conditions that can be changed.

3. Specific attention should be given to long-range and project planning which can help reduce employee anxiety.

4. In project management, a system for phasing projects effectively is needed. Personnel transfer policies as well as interproject training programs will be a useful part of this system.

5. As was stressed in Chapter 7, free-flowing two-way communication is one of the major factors that influences the quality of the organizational climate.

Vroom and Yetton have developed a decision-process flow chart, which offers great promise to engineering managers in determining the proper points on the autocratic-democratic continuum given the nature of the decision.[13] While a detailed analysis will not be made of the Vroom and Yetton approach, it is useful to indicate some pertinent questions which when answered help determine the extent of democracy needed in the decision-making process. Among these more important questions are as follows:

Do I have enough information to make a high-quality decision? Obviously, the more managers depend on others for information, the more consultative or democratic they need to be.

Is acceptance of a decision by subordinates critical to effective implementation? If the answer to this question is yes, it is more important to be democratic than if the answer is no.

If I were to make the decision by myself, is it reasonably certain that it would be accepted by my subordinates? If the answer is yes, then it is less important to be on the democratic side of the continuum.

Do subordinates share the organizational goals to be attained in solving this problem? If the answer is yes, then subordinates can effectively become more involved in the decision process than if the answer is no.

Do subordinates have sufficient information to make a high-quality decision? If the answer is yes, managers can be more democratic than if the answer is no.

The preceding questions posed by Vroom and Yetton are critical ones that technical managers should answer before attempting to arrive at the amount of participation or consultation that should be afforded to subordinates in the decision-making process. These questions also relate to many of the critical factors that determine proper position along the continuum depicted in Figure 9.1. The commitment of subordinates to the problem, the time involved, sharing of goals, and the general level of cooperation and communication among the subordinates are all good measures of organizational climate and basic factors that determine the best leadership style.

Emotional Styles of the Leader

An additional important factor that impacts on the choice of an appropriate leadership style is the value system, personality, and emotional style of the leader. Research conducted by the National Training Laboratories and reported by Athos and Coffey clearly identifies three emotional styles.[14] A slightly modified version of these three styles and their basic characteristics is contained in Figure 9.2. As this figure indicates, these three styles are the sturdy battler, the friendly helper, and the logical thinker. While no individual is totally classified as one style or the other, many people tend to express or feel comfortable with one type more than another.[15] In view of the distinguishable characteristics that are associated with each of these three styles, it is clear that each emotional style will influence to a greater or lesser degree an individual's approach to leadership and management.

It must still be emphasized that leadership can be learned and a technical manager can be taught to change his or her approach to leadership, but the emotional style of that specific manager can determine the degree of comfort experienced in practicing a given style. There are other implications regarding emotional style that are also important to a full understanding of leadership. For example, specific managers who are predominantly "sturdy battler" types may succeed with autocracy in situations were leaders with different emotional styles would fail as autocrats. This difference is explained by the fact that sturdy battlers are often more comfortable and effective when assuming an autocratic role.

Similarly, individuals who are predominantly "friendly helper" types often succeed in a wide variety of situations with democratic leadership because they are very sincere and comfortable with it. Friendly helpers thrive on warm, supportive relationships which are fostered by a democratic philosophy. Since autocratic leadership is often not seen as being warm and supportive, the friendly helper feels awkward in situations that call for "hard-nosed" boss-centered decisions.

Finally, since bureaucracy is characterized by formal rules and regulations that are based on logic, accuracy, and knowledge, the bureaucratic leadership style can be very appealing to "logical thinker" types. These leaders are most comfortable when a logical system exists which can be used to support their decisions; consequently, they are often prone to managing bureaucratically, whereas others with different emotional styles are not.

Technical managers should determine their own emotional style and analyze how it is affecting their leadership practices. Although it is common to find that effectiveness is greatest when using a leadership pattern that is congruent with one's emotional style, this may only be true when the characteristics of the situation dictate the use of that style. If the characteristics of the situation suggest another approach, effectiveness will be reduced. Technical managers that are predominantly sturdy battlers should realize that they are prone to being

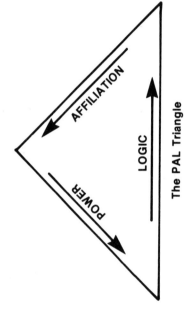

The PAL Triangle

The Friendly Helper

a. uncomfortable with tough emotions
b. comfortable with tender emotions — avoids conflict and freely expresses warmth and support
c. tends to evaluate others on the basis of supporting relationships
d. prefers democracy in leadership situations

The Sturdy Battler

a. uncomfortable with tender emotions
b. comfortable with tough emotions — often thrives on conflict
c. evaluates others in terms of their power and ability to control
d. often prefers autocracy in leadership situations

The Logical Thinker

a. uncomfortable with both tough and tender emotions
b. relies heavily on knowledge and accuracy
c. evaluates others in terms of their knowledge and expertise
d. is often comfortable with bureaucratic leadership

Figure 9.2 Basic emotional styles that are associated with individuals performing leadership roles

autocratic; those who are friendly helpers are more likely to be democratic; and logical thinkers may tend toward bureaucratic leadership regardless of the situation. In important decision-making situations, these managers should make a crtical appraisal of the extent to which their own emotional style may be influencing them to apply an inappropriate leadership pattern. Technical managers can and should be taught that flexibility in the application of leadership style is important.

Relationship Between Power and Leadership

Since power can be defined as the capacity to change behavior, many authorities on leadership believe that the power position of the leader with regard to subordinates is a critical factor in determining leadership effectiveness.[16] French and Raven have described five different power bases that are available to leaders in given organizational situations which are outlined below:[17]

Coercive power: This is based upon fear and relates primarily to the ability of the leader to punish the subordinates for nonconformity.

Reward power: This is the opposite of coercive power in the sense that it relates to the ability of the leader to provide positive rewards, such as income or other benefits to people who cooperate.

Legitimate power: This type of power relates to the position of the manager in the organizational hierarchy and is largely derived from the ability of the organization to support that manager in terms of his or her organizational position.

Expert power: An individual with this type of power is one who possesses unique expertise or skills in particular areas that are regarded as important to subordinates.

Referrent power: This is essentially the power of the personality and relates to the leader's ability to be admired because of one or more personal traits.

Each of these power bases is limited in scope by the nature of the organization and the person occupying a leadership position. For example, legitimate power is limited by the scope of the office as defined by the job description covering duties and responsibilities as well as the financial strength, prestige, and size of the organization. Expert power is usually restricted to those situations where expertise is valued by the subordinates; therefore, attempts to carry it into other situations usually is not successful. Reward power is often dictated by the financial strength and size of the organization as well as the autonomy given to the manager by top management. It follows that high level managers in powerful organizations usually have more rewards to provide than lower level managers in smaller organizations. Likewise, the impact of a Civil Service System or a union on reward and coercive power requires little explanation. Researchers working for governmental agencies covered by Civil Service requirements are somewhat limited in their ability to discharge, promote, or grant other kinds of rewards or punishments to their subordinates. Many managers who are subjected to these artificial restrictions maintain that their ability to be effective leaders is greatly reduced.

The important message for practical leadership from an analysis of power is simply that an effective manager needs power to influence subordinates. More powerful managers have greater freedom in chosing a leadership style. Technical managers should not only develop their bases of power, but they should be willing to use those power bases as needs arise. For example, regardless of leadership style practiced, if an engineering manager is unwilling to exercise punishment when subordinates do not cooperate, the managerial power base is being eroded. At the same time, a manager who rewards all employees the same, regardless of their level of performance, is eroding the reward power base and reducing total managerial power.

Specific studies of the engineering and scientific work environment have found position power to be primarily determined by organizational climate rather than by type of organization.[18] Position power is usually not influenced by either matrix or functional organizational structuring, but can be strong in both structures with supportive overall climates. While the effectiveness of a technical manager's leadership style is influenced by his or her position power, the appropriate choice of a particular style depends primarily on the organizational climate. The characteristics of good and poor climates were delineated earlier in this chapter.

Effective Technical Managers Are Good Helpers

Every leader during the course of managing people must assume a helping role, but knowing the proper way to be helpful is a complex matter. A basic part of good leadership is problem solving, but if the leader solves all subordinate problems, he or she keeps others dependent and does not develop subordinates.

The specific role of effective helping should be to teach others to solve their own problems. Constructive helping directs a person toward self-help. However, much too often the motives for helping people are not directed toward self-help, but are aimed at some self-serving purpose for the leader-manager. Some of the questionable motives for helping are:

To obtain gratitude or raise guilt

To make the subordinate happy

To give meaning to the leader's life

To show one's superior skill as a person

To control others or make them dependent

All of these particular motives for helping tend to breed defensive actions or attitudes on the part of the subordinate that is destructive to organizational effectiveness. If subordinates do not openly resent or become apathetic about help that occurs in this context, they may tend to feel helpless and become very dependent upon the leader. Any of these conditions impedes the ability of the organization to move forward and utilize subordinates properly in the attainment of organizational goals. The manager of engineering and scientific personnel will often find a challenging problem in knowing when, how long, and how intensely to help subordinates solve problems.

Pitfalls to Avoid in Building a Proper Helping Relationship with Subordinates

There are several specific pitfalls that should be avoided by technical managers who desire to build a constructive, helpful relationship with subordinates. Some of the most important ones are outlined below:

Avoid providing early advice to subordinates; instead, assume a stance that is problem centered. Giving advice is often both inappropriate and ineffective for two reasons. First, it is assumed that the leader understands the subordinate's problem and has the correct advice, but this is often not true. Even with sound advice, the manager has solved the problem for the subordinate, which tends to make the subordinate more dependent. Secondly, even good advice often breeds rejection. Most professional people want to solve their own problems rather than have the manager solve those problems for them.

Avoid excessive use of reassurance or "pat-on-the-back" approaches. The problem with these kinds of approaches is that their effectiveness is very short-lived. In essence, they deny that a problem exists when in reality this assumption may be incorrect. These approaches are commonly used by managers because they create good feeling, but their success record is poor. The subordinate can find himself or herself in the position of after being encouraged and told everything is going to be all right for a period of months, they are suddenly in deeper trouble.

Avoid using punitive measures as a means of correcting deviant behavior or to get people on the prescribed course toward solving problems. Punishment tends to breed a considerable amount of defensiveness and rejection; consequently, it often reduces the problem-solving ability of both the manager and the subordinate. Unless there have been specific instances where willful violation of rules and costly mistakes were made with questionable intent, one should avoid punishing subordinates for things that they do not understand or have not yet mastered. Many managers feel that correction of errors is the best disciplinary procedure they have available, and they seldom go into actual punitive measures. Correction of errors assumes that the subordinate does not understand how to deal with the problem and it sets in motion forces to teach the subordinate the proper way to deal with the problem at a future time. It is not until there is willful, costly violation to the company by subordinates that strong disciplinary measures are taken.

Avoid making subordinates look bad in front of their peers. When employees are making mistakes which need to be corrected, discussion and attempts to solve these problems should be conducted in private, and not in front of other co-workers. Public ridicule is an ultimate example of criticism and lowering one's self-esteem in the eyes of others, which has been stressed throughout this book as one of the biggest single mistakes an effective technical manager can make.

Avoid favoritism. If a superior is willing to help some subordinates but not others, both cooperation and motivation suffer. Constructive, supportive help should be available on an equal basis to all subordinates, and each of these subordinates should feel that the opportunity for such help is available to them when they need it.

Avoid bailing subordinates out of trouble too quickly. The overall objective of the effective helper is to get the subordinate to rescue himself or herself. This is the key to building a strong team characterized by self-confidence, self-esteem, and problem-solving skills. A certain amount of struggling on the part of the subordinate is often necessary and useful in attaining this objective.

Action Steps That Will Aid the Helping Relationship

There are several positive steps that technical managers can take to build strong, helping relationships. Some of the more useful are as follows:

1. Focus on the problem, not the person. The goal should be to help the person understand the problem. Effective helping is based on the assumption that the only person that can really solve the problem is the person experiencing it.

2. Ask questions that help keep subordinates focused on the problem. It is particularly useful to ask what solutions have been tried and why they did not work.

3. Allow subordinates to explain their feelings and attitudes about the problem situation, thereby increasing the probability that accurate perceptions of the problem will occur.

4. Empathy is important, but too much empathizing can be detrimental to an objective perception of the problem.

5. Once the subordinate accepts and accurately perceives the nature of the problem, provide available tools and support to expedite a solution. For example, if it is secretarial help, typing assistance, transportation, or time off from the job that is needed, the effective helper-manager provides it. This kind of support impacts favorably on subordinates' perceptions of their bosses, develops interpersonal problem-solving skills, and reduces conflict.

Summary and Conclusions

This chapter has identified and emphasized the importance of choosing an appropriate leadership style for managerial effectiveness in the technical environment. While innate characteristics influence the capacity to lead, many leadership qualities are learned or acquired. This fact adds credibility to the study of leadership. Choosing an appropriate leadership style in technical management is a function of the manager, subordinates, and situation. Several aids have been provided that will assist the technical manager to correctly analyze the total leadership environment. Two basic guidelines are useful in making this analysis. First, it is important to be doing the right things rather than to worry constantly about doing things right. Second, the emphasis should be on being effective as opposed to being efficient.

Effective managers level with subordinates and minimize both game playing and the use of formal rules and regulations as control devices. Straight talk is valued by most professional people, such as engineers and scientists, and it tends to keep a more realistic focus on the organizational environment and the objectives, which is often the key to leadership effectiveness. Good technical managers continually review and focus on objectives as well as the problems that subordinates are encountering in attaining those objectives. Development of a problem-solving attitude through proper helping and mutual support is the key to accomplishing meaningful results.

While this chapter has stressed that several variables affect the choice of style, a great many managerial situations in the technical environment dictate a democratic approach. High levels of professionalism and self-discipline among these employees are basic factors that suggest democracy. Also, democratic management that utilizes communication feedback principles can be very helpful in developing mutual support with subordinates. Democratic leadership allows the boss to be perceived as helping his or her subordinates get the work done, rather than being perceived as being served by subordinates, which is an ineffective attitude to have permeating the research and engineering environment. Technical managers are often rated on their helpfulness in reaching goals for subordinates that relate to total organizational objectives, rather than on their own specific intelligence or skills as individuals. Managers who use superior intelligence and skill to make themselves look good, hoping that this goodness will rub off on subordinates, are much less likely to be perceived as effective managers than managers who use intelligence and skill to build problem-solving skills and self-esteem among their subordinates.

Finally, the key to managerial effectiveness resides in the organizational climate. While some elements of climate are outside the control of the manager, there are many elements that can be modified and improved. The improvement of overall organizational climate should be a high priority goal of all technical managers.

Notes

1. Simon Marcson, Role Concept of Engineering Managers. *IRE Transactions on Engineering Management,* March 1960, pp. 30-33.

2. Rensis Likert, Motivation: The Core of Management. *American Management Association,* Personnel Series no. 155, 1953, pp. 3-21.

3. Rensis Likert, Human Resource Accounting: Building and Assessing Productive Organizations. *Personnel,* May-June 1973, pp. 8-24.

4. Jacob B. Paperman and Desmond D. Martin, Human Resource Accounting: A Managerial Tool. *Personnel,* vol. 54, no. 2, March-April 1977, pp. 41-50.

5. Donald C. Pelz, Influence: A Key to Effective Leadership in the First Line Supervisor. *Personnel,* vol. 29, 1952, pp. 209-217.

6. Victor A. Thompson, *Modern Organization,* Alfred A. Knopf, New York, 1961, pp. 152-169.

7. Donald C. Pelz and F. M. Andrews, *Scientists in Organizations: Productive Climates for Research and Development,* University of Michigan Institute for Social Research, Ann Arbor, Mich., 1976, p. 7.

8. Chester Barnard, *The Functions of the Executive,* Harvard University Press, Cambridge, Mass., 1938, pp. 161-163.

9. For a discussion of Lewin's work, see Ronald O. Lippitt and Ralph K. White, The Social Climate of Childrens Groups, in *Child Behavior and Development* (R. G. Barker, ed.), McGraw-Hill, New York, 1943, pp.485-508.

10. Hans J. Thamhain and David L. Wilemon, Leadership Effectiveness in Program Management. *IEEE Transactions on Engineering Management,* vol. EM24, no. 3, August 1977, pp. 102-108.

11. *Ibid.*

12. *Ibid.*

13. Victor H. Vroom and Philip W. Yetton, *Leadership and Decision Making,* University of Pittsburgh Press, Pittsburgh, 1973.

14. Anthony G. Athos and Robert E. Coffey, *Behavior In Organizations: A Multidimensional View,* Prentice-Hall, Englewood Cliffs, N.J., 1975, p. 119.

15. *Ibid.,* p. 118.

16. Fred E. Fiedler, *A Theory of Leadership Effectiveness,* McGraw-Hill, New York, 1967, p. 142.

17. J. R. P. French, Jr. and B. Raven, The Bases of Social Power, in *Studies in Social Power* (Dorwin Cartwright, ed.), University of Michigan Press, Ann Arbor, Mich., 1959, pp. 150-167.

18. Thamhain and Wilemon, "Leadership Effectiveness in Program Management."

10 Effective Management
of the Change Process

Importance and Nature of Change

One of the most perplexing problems that confronts technical managers is the problem of dealing with change, namely, the successful introduction of change in the organizational environment. Change is a management problem, because managers are usually the people who desire that changes be made for the purpose of increasing the ability of the organization to attain its goals.

The current business environment is so competitive that changes must be made constantly if the organization is to adapt and be effective. In studies of organizational effectiveness in recent years, adaptability and flexibility continually show up among the top three or four variables that impact on effectiveness as perceived by practicing managers.[1] Adaptability and flexibility are integral parts of the change process. Managers in the engineering and scientific environment are most concerned with change because the ability of the firm to adapt often rests with the engineering, research and development, and scientific staff that are normally associated with an enterprise. While engineers may be more prone to accept change because of their level of education and accomplishment, unless they are properly managed they can be just as resistant to change as other employee groups.

For the purpose of analysis, change is defined as any alteration in the established way of doing things. According to this definition, change does not necessarily have to involve a change in technology or employees; a simple modification in work location within a given work environment can cause the same types of management problems as those caused by larger or more apparent changes. If all changes were readily accepted, resistance would not be a problem to engineering and scientific managers; but change is often resisted which results in increased costs as well as causing managers both psychological and technological problems of adjustment.

The authors have observed instances where employees' desks were moved away from a window and productivity dropped sharply. Since the supervision and tasks assigned remained the same, the only thing that had changed was the arrangement of the desks in the room. Although in cases of this kind resistance has an impact on management problems, to the outside observer it is difficult to discern that any change has been made at all. Thus, it is not always major changes in technology, supervision, or task that cause supervisory problems.

Three Phases of Change

While there are several frameworks for examining resistance to change, an examination of the three phases or stages of the change process will aid our understanding. Since the primary concern of most managers is to reduce employee resistance and increase efficiency, it is important to realize that resistance can occur during any one of the three specific phases or stages that accompany every organizational change. Specifically, these three phases are the threat, impact, and after-effects of change.[2] The ability of the technical manager to plan for change, anticipate problems before they become costly, and understand the present stage of the specific change can be a major factor in determining managerial effectiveness.

Threat Phase

The *threat phase* of change is that time period during which a rumor moves through the informal (grapevine) or regular management channels that suggests that a change is possible or likely to be imposed. A threat phase may occur even though the change never actually happens. If employees believe that such a change will happen, they can start resisting it immediately. Employees may quit their jobs or lower their productivity long before a change ever actually takes place. These negative responses by employees are a result of the fact that they believe that a change is actually coming or contemplated. The length of time and significance of the threat phase is determined by the speed and the size of the change. Changes that are made quickly obviously have a very short threat phase. Changes that are large and require a considerable amount of planning usually have a threat phase of a year or more. Examples of these latter types of change include changes in building location, alterations involving automation or technology improvements, or a major change in work procedure. These changes are usually perceived to be significant by employees, require long lead times, and consequently may have a long threat phase. The technical manager's ability to deal properly with the threat phase has a direct influence on both the nature and extent of resistance encountered. Involving subordinates in change planning, being frank and honest about probable impact in answering questions, and not making misleading promises to employees are important elements of the sound management of change.

Impact Phase

The second phase of change, which is commonly referred to as the *impact phase*, occurs when the organizational change is implemented. Often technical managers get through the threat phase without difficulty because the company has a good reputation for changes in the past or because they have explained the nature of the change adequately. Once the change is introduced, however, serious problems may confront these managers. Why? Many times when people are actually trying a new process or building new work relationships, they find that it is actually more difficult than they first realized, and they then begin resisting the change. Also, these subordinates find that after the change is actually introduced, many of its aspects that they thought would be insignificant in the planning phase actually turn out to be much more threatening than was originally believed. This situation calls for appropriate managerial action designed to minimize the inefficiencies due to resistant behavior by employees. Increased attention needs to be given to communication with subordinates so their true problems with the change can be fully understood.

After-effect Phase

The *after-effect phase* of change can involve resistance for several months, a year, or even longer after the change has apparently been introduced successfully. Employees sometimes accept the impact phase of change simply because it is a new, stimulating activity that is different from their previous work assignments. Unfortunately, however, the newness wears off, and 3 or 4 months after a change has been introduced, workers may decide that they would prefer to have the old way back again. Resistance in the form of poor workmanship, increased conflict, or lack of tolerance for fellow workers may occur. Thus, the change process is usually long term, particularly for larger changes. In fact, the after-effects phase may occur over a period of several years from the time the change is first contemplated until it has been fully integrated and accepted into the organization. Due to the many factors that lead to filtering communication that were discussed in Chapter 7, employees may not tell their managers the real problem. Since these managers do not associate sloppy effort or declining morale with a change made several months earlier, it is not surprising that the after-effects phase can be the most troublesome and difficult to resolve. When a change in subordinate effectiveness occurs for no apparent reason, the technical manager should seek an answer to the following question: *Have any significant changes been made during the past 2 years that could be influencing my subordinates negatively?* If the answer is yes, open communication can be helpful in getting to the root of the problem.

Nature of Resistance to Change

Managers need to understand the nature of resistance to change in order to reduce its harmful effects in the managerial environment. Many engineering and scientific managers believe that there is a natural tendency to resist change, but there is little evidence that this is true. A major point of Alvin Toffler's popular book, *Future Shock,* is that changes are taking place faster in our society than we can adjust to them.[3] Our society is characterized by rapid change, and a cursory examination of observable events indicates that change is eventually accepted. The effective manager works to minimize the time needed for the acceptance of change.

Causes of Resistance to Change

All organizational changes are not accepted, and therefore managers must frequently deal with problems of resistance to change. A common cause of this resistance in the technical environment is fear; specifically, fear of what the change will do to the individuals that have to work with the change. Managerial action that increases understanding reduces fear and increases acceptance.

Changes that are perceived by employees to lower their social status in the organization tend to be resisted. In the previously mentioned case in which the desks were moved away from the windows, the windows were status symbols to the employees in that specific work environment. When they were moved away from the windows, employees who worked at those desks perceived that their status was being lowered in the organization, and they became resistant and their productivity suffered. The management was totally unaware of the important relationship between window location and desk placement. Thus, feelings of self-worth are often influenced by subtle changes, and employees vehemently resist changes that threaten their self-worth. The methods used by specific managers in introducing changes can have as much of an impact on employee perceptions of self-worth as the changes themselves.[4] It is also true that employees may have a genuine concern and feeling of insecurity which occupies their minds when changes take place that cause the environment to appear unstable. Under these circumstances, these employees often do not fully realize the impact of their reaction on those around them. Methods that provide consideration of employee feelings are very helpful in minimizing these kinds of perception problems.

Changes that upset valued social relationships tend to be resisted. As indicated in Chapter 8 on motivation, social needs are often strong needs, and when changes are made that upset social realtionships and frustrate these needs, they will be resisted. Employee needs for security are also strong. When changes are made that are perceived to be threatening either to an employee's physical or economic security, they will be vehemently resisted. Technical managers should ask themselves the following question before an attempt is made to integrate change in work environment: What will this change do to (1) the status of the employees affected by the change, (2) the social relationships of the employees affected by the change, and (3) the economic and physical security of the employees? If the change has a negative impact on any one of these three variables, then management can predict with a high degree of certainty that these changes will be resisted. Managers of technical and staff specialists such as engineers often overlook the psychological effects of change that appear to be logical and are unprepared for the resistance that follows.[5] In addition, studies have shown that technical specialists often resist changes that do not originate in their own departments.[6] Apparently, these specialists view orginating ideas as an idex of departmental status and strive to protect the status image of their departments by rejecting outside ideas. This rejection can be troublesome because it usually is not based on the true value of the proposal. Successful technical managers will attempt to minimize this resistance either by eliminating its cause or by some way minimizing its importance to the employees. Emphasizing the value of cooperation with outside individuals and units to the ultimate well being of the engineering group can be helpful in stimulating greater acceptance of outside ideas and proposals.

It has been pointed out that change can be considered from two points of view, namely, the change agent or manager who implements the change and the people (subordinates) affected by the change. Much of the practical and theoretical emphasis has been on change agents and how they may best implement proposed changes. The implicit assumption often is that employees have little capability to accept or express positive responses toward planned change. This assumption may cause managers to anticipate resistance from employees which may lead to resistant behavior that would not ordinarily occur.[7] Specifically, managers focus so strongly on probable resistance that employees respond as they feel they are expected to, namely, to resist the proposed change. These managerial assumptions are often both unwise and unwarranted.

Specific Methods and Techniques for Reducing Resistance

Considerable attention has been directed toward proper ways of introducing change so that resistance is overcome. Many techniques have proven value in the engineering and scientific environment. Often fears of status or security loss or destruction of social relationships are imaginary. In these cases, introducing employee participation into the change process can be vital in reducing resistance to the change. As discussed in Chapter 9, democratic leadership is helpful for technical managers when these kinds of situations are present. Resistance to change can be reduced if the manager can sell through participation the idea that employees will be better off as a result of making the change. As shown in Figure 10.1, unless the forces for acceptance are clearly greater

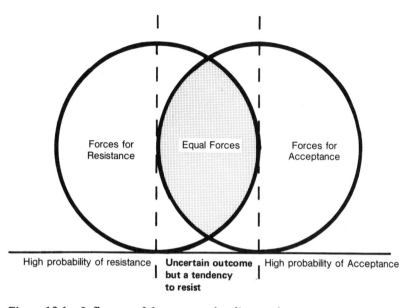

Figure 10.1   Influence of forces on subordinates that suggest acceptance of or resistance to proposed changes

than those for resistance, the probability of employees resisting the change is high. The extent and direction of these forces are determined by several variables. The more important of these variables are the manager, organizational climate, work group attitudes, employee value systems, and the change itself. Sometimes the technical manager can use participation to impact favorably on enough of these variables so employees perceive that a net gain will result from making the change. If the manager is successful with participation, in the context of Figure 10.1, the forces favoring the change would exceed the forces against the change, and resistance will be alleviated as a managerial problem.

The process of getting employee acceptance often involves creating a "we" attitude in making changes. A "we" attitude can result from employee involvement through democratic management. Ideally, employees should feel that part of the substance of the change is their own idea. This is not as difficult as it may at first sound, because managerially promoted changes are usually desirable for the organization, and as the organization benefits, more rewards are available to the individual employee. Many times it is clear that a change is going to yield direct benefits to employees, e.g., create better research or engineering facilities, more pleasant working conditions, or modernized equipment. In these instances participation effectively reduces employee resistance, because understanding increases the strength of the forces for acceptance.

Resistant employee attitudes do not automatically yield resistant behavior, because attitudes of colleagues and the overall work group often keep employees from expressing their true feelings. Technical managers that can convince informal group leaders of the need for proposed changes can minimize the impact of resistant attitudes by specific employees. Employees are unlikely to exhibit resistant behavior if it is not supported by the groups in which membership is valued. As pointed out in Chapter 6, cohesive work groups can exercise great control over the expression of individual employee attitudes. In effect one of the strongest "we" attitudes that is potentially available to engineering and scientific managers consists of the development of a favorable overall group attitude toward proposed changes.

Creating a "we" attitude involves the willingness to compromise on the part of management. For example, a manager discusses with a group of engineers the idea of introducing several new machines into the work process and meets with some resistance such as a suggestion from the group that one particular machine should not be purchased as previously planned. This suggestion should be honored if practical. The "we" attitude emerges when the engineering manager responds positively to these kinds of requests, because the manager is perceived to be both responsive and supportive through this sincere compromise effort, and the engineering or scientific subordinates see that they are impacting on the change process. Conversely, the engineering manager who invites his subordinates in for suggestions on changes and gets several suggestions for corrections and modifications but ignores them loses credibility and the valuable "we" attitude very quickly.

Several research studies including the classic Coch and French study of the late 1940s support the fact that change by decree is likely to meet with a great deal of resistance.[8] For instance, Coch and French had changes introduced by three possible methods in a manufacturing environment as follows: First, all subordinates were involved in the change on a total participation basis. Second, employees selected representatives from their group to meet with management and discuss the change. Third, the changes were introduced by decree or with no participation. In surveying the results of the three particular methods, these researchers found that there was less resistance exhibited by the group that experienced total participation. Apparently, a "we" attitude ensued which had beneficial effects. Introducing change by decree caused the most resistance among the three methods. Autocratic change often destroys the "we" attitude, and unless the change is clearly seen as favorable, employees will resist it.

Certain types of decisions that involve organizational change are inappropriate for participation and subordinate involvement. For example, when a manager is faced with decisions involving employee layoffs (staff reductions) or disciplinary action against specific employees, it is usually not fair or useful to involve subordinates in these sensitive matters. In simple terms, increasing understanding and involvement through participation will not increase the forces for acceptance of these kinds of changes (see Figure 10.1). However, it is often helpful to obtain employee participation in the formulation of policies guiding layoff or disciplinary procedures prior to implementation.

Task Force Concept

Major changes in the technical environment can often be integrated effectively with the use of the *task force*. This concept simply involves appointing a task force of key subordinate engineers and managers to study problems where changes are needed and to recommend the nature and content of changes to be made. Three important steps are necessary in making task forces work. First, select key group leaders for the task force. These employees should have the respect and support of their coworkers, and should have proven performance records. Second, use democratic techniques in managing the task force so all members will become involved and committed. Third, once the task force makes a recommendation for change, allow it to continue as a unit to play a key role in implementation.

The positive results from following these steps will be that major changes are often integrated effectively into the organization with a minimum of conflict. Obviously, the change must be of significant size and impact so that the cost of formulating and implementing the task force will be worthwhile. Many engineering changes that involve equipment purchases, new work procedures, or new product lines, where the focus of employee activities must be changed, are particularly suited for task force assignment. If the task force is formed early during major changes, especially when the change is initially contemplated, the threat phase of the change is often dealt with more effectively. The task force can gather data, field questions, and solicit input so that employees understand and become more involved in what is going to be done. This involvement is particularly important to engineering and scientific employees.

What to Do When Participation Does Not Work

In addition to layoffs and cases involving disciplinary action, there are other changes that, no matter how much participation is involved, the employee cannot see that an improved personal position will result from making the change. In these situations there are two avenues available to the technical manager. One is to use other compensating factors to offset the employee's perceived negative impact of the change. Some possible compensating factors are discussed below.

First, increasing the level of pay to the employees affected and thereby reducing their dissatisfaction; second, increasing the amount of fringe benefits or privileges such as travel opportunities or vacation time; and third, making changes in the physical environment, such as improved facilities or adding to support staff. The amount of control the technical manager has over many of the above factors varies greatly from one organization to another and within a given firm. However, managers usually have some influence on one or more of these areas (often more than they realize), and the important point is to use it wisely. Compensating for the negative aspects of the change by increasing some of the hygiene factors or improving intrinsic job factors is useful in off-setting negative attitudes about given changes. This approach costs money, and the cost has to be weighed against the benefits received. The key question for the manager to ask is as follows: *Are the costs of resistance going to outweigh the costs of providing these extra compensatory factors?* A positive or negative answer should determine the course of action.

A second approach to reducing resistance when change is perceived negatively and participation is not working is to introduce change on a tentative basis. When making changes on a tentative basis, technical managers should obtain employee agreement to try the changes, but if the changes turn out to be disruptive and dissatisfying, they also collectively agree to withdraw the change. If the tentative change concept is to work, managers must be able to reverse decisions regarding change. Consequently, if a change is made that management does not believe is reversible, it should not be made on a tentative basis. Technical managers should realize that their integrity is at stake in the change process, and to agree to do things and then not follow through destroys managerial effectiveness. Managers should not agree to make changes with employees that are impossible, or make other promises simply to get acceptance of a change. Engineers and scientists will not respect a manager that says one thing and does another. Even proven methods of introducing change such as participation should not be undertaken unless the manager values participation and intends to utilize the input provided by the subordinates. In view of these facts, technical managers should be careful about how they handle the change process. Specifically, the change situation should be analyzed carefully before changes are made, and then one of the particular approaches outlined in this chapter may be applied.

Summary

Many factors and concepts have been analyzed in this chapter that impact on resistance to change. A summary is outlined below:

1. Changes are not automatically resisted, but employees must perceive that there are distinct advantages to making a change in order to avoid resistant behavior.

2. Since resistant attitudes by individual employees do not necessarily lead to resistant behavior because of environmental pressures, it is important for technical managers to work with group leadership in order to overcome specific employee resistances. If employees value their group relationships, which is common among engineering and scientific employees, they will be reluctant to resist changes that have overall group support. Engineering managers will find that informal group leadership can be an important ally in making changes.

3. The extent of employees' trust in management coupled with their own sense of security impacts strongly on acceptance or rejection of change.

4. Resistance to change can occur during any one of three specific phases of the change process.

5. Changes that are not understood often become clouded by employee perception of fear and uncertainty, which leads directly to resistant behavior.

6. Changes that threaten job skills or are perceived to impact negatively on job content or status factors important to the engineering staff are likely to result in resistant behavior.

7. While participation in the change process is one of the most useful ways of reducing resistance, there are several types of change problems where it is ineffective. Management's provision for additional remuneration or making the change tentative can help reduce resistance when participation is not enough.

8. The task force concept is an important vehicle for implementing change.

9. Managers should support promises with action, because management credibility is an important factor in determining the nature and extent of resistance.

Notes

1. Richard Steers, Problems in the Measurement of Organizational Effectiveness. *Administrative Science Quarterly,* vol. 20, 1975, pp. 564-558.

2. Irving L. Janis, Problems of Theory in the Analysis of Stress Behavior. *Journal of Social Issues,* Summer 1954, pp. 12-25.

3. Alvin Toffler, *Future Shock,* Bantam Books, New York, 1971, p. 259.

4. Bidu Shekhar Jha, Resistant to Change—How to Overcome. *Industrial Management,* May-June 1977, pp. 21-22.

5. Keith Davis, *Human Behavior at Work,* McGraw-Hill, New York, 1977, p. 165.

6. Melville Dalton, Changing Life Staff Relationships. *Personnel Administration,* vol. 29, no. 2, March-April 1966, pp. 40-48.

7. Gary Powell and Barry Posuer, Resistance to Change Reconsidered: Implications for Managers. *Human Resource Management,* vol. 17, no. 1, Spring 1978, pp. 29-34.

8. Lester Coch and John R. P. French, Jr., Overcoming Resistance to Change. *Human Relations,* vol. 1, no. 4, 1948, pp. 512-532.

11 Management by Objectives: A Successful Tool for Integrating Participation and Control

Introduction

The pioneering work begun in the 1950s by Peter F. Drucker and George S. Odiorne, two outstanding management scholars, in developing an approach to management known as *management by objective's* or MBO, is now being given increasing amounts of consideration by both academicians and the management practitioner.[1] It is based on two fundamental premises: First, the clearer the idea one has of what one is trying to do, the greater the chance of accomplishing it; and second, progress can only be measured in terms of what one is trying to make progress toward. This approach to management, which establishes clearcut objectives throughout the organization and then evaluates participants on how well they attain objectives that are based on mutual agreement between superiors and subordinates, seems to offer great promise to technical managers who are attempting to increase their division's effectiveness. Also, since most engineering and research departments must compete for funds with other organizational units that consistently seek dollar increases in their operating budgets, the development of clearcut division performance objectives can be a useful bargaining tool to help assure attainment of a "fair share." This modern management tool has been either partially or totally adopted in many areas of both private and public enterprise. Since MBO has superiors and subordinates at all levels setting goals together and working to achieve these goals in a cooperative fashion, it has produced highly satisfactory results in many organizations.

In a recent study, 300 American personnel managers of firms employing 1000 or more were asked to rank six widely known management tools according to their perception of the ability of the proper application of these tools to increase organizational effectiveness.[2] These six tools and their respective rankings by the 165 personnel managers that responded including mean values are as follows:

1. Management by objectives (2.4)

2. Human relations training (as part of formalized management development (3.0)

3. Management information systems (3.1)

4. Skill training (as part of the personnel program) (3.6)

5. PERT (performance evaluation and review technique) (4.0)

6. Human resource accounting (4.9)

Management by objectives was clearly the preferred tool among personnel managers which reflects the sustained popularity of MBO since its inception in the mid 1950s. Both the high rankings of MBO and human relations training may in part reflect the strong people orientation of the type of managers surveyed. Also, this finding may in part reflect more recognition or knowledge of this tool than some of the others. For example, if production managers or engineering managers were asked this same question, one could expect both management information systems and PERT to be given considerably more importance, both due to greater knowledge and perceived applicability to their function. Since recent research indicates that human resource accounting is not currently being practiced in any organization, it is not surprising that it would rank last among these six tools.[3]

In addition to the influence of people orientation on the favorable perceptions of personnel managers toward MBO, it is likely that these same attitudes influence these perceptions concerning the way goals are set among superiors and subordinates in their respective organizations. Over 90 percent of these managers see that goals are established only after some solicitation of input or some agreement is attained among the parties involved. Less than 10 percent of these managers see goals being set autocratically by management decree. These perceptions might be quite different among managers with less people orientation such as line production managers, maintenance managers, or plant superintendents.

These findings are important to engineering managers because personnel managers often strongly influence the basic management philosophy of the organization. It is clear that these managers tend to favor MBO and mutual goal setting and will likely encourage engineering and scientific units to move in that direction.

What MBO Has to Offer

One researcher found that in an engineering and research environment a direct relationship existed between experiencing ambiguity and job tension, job dissatisfaction, personal ineffectiveness, and unfavorable attitudes toward work associates; and suggested that a program of MBO would be appropriate for reducing both ambiguity and conflict.[4] Once understood, MBO is often welcomed by both managers and subordinates alike because it is a management system based on cooperation, communication, and participation by all levels in the organization, and all organizational participants can realize benefits. In fact, MBO is essentially a system wherein supervisors and subordinates participate in objective setting, work toward the objectives, and realize satisfaction as goals are reached.

To illustrate how MBO differs from traditional organizational approaches to management, Figure 11.1 compares a typical classical approach to management with the more behavioristic approach of MBO. Note how in conventional management authority is vested in the positions themselves in the organization. This situation is depicted by the heavy lines which enclose the squares which represent the position levels in the hierarchy. Likewise, the authority arrow flows from the top down, emphasizing the dictatorial approach, in which there is little room for collective objective setting which capitalizes on the talents of subordinates. However, note how the identical organization changes with the distinct shift in emphasis of MBO. Heavy lines indicate that now the emphasis is in the level between positions, the level where objectives are jointly set by superiors and subordinates. The authority arrow has a head at the top as well as at the bottom, indicating the communication feedback process which superiors can use for better and stronger decisions

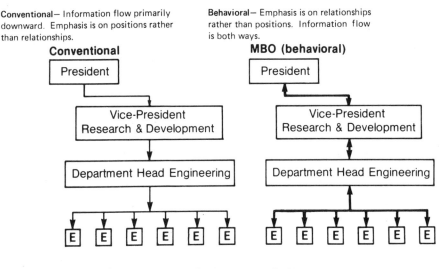

Conventional— Information flow primarily downward. Emphasis is on positions rather than relationships.

Behavioral— Emphasis is on relationships rather than positions. Information flow is both ways.

Conventional

President

Vice-President Research & Development

Department Head Engineering

E E E E E E

MBO (behavioral)

President

Vice-President Research & Development

Department Head Engineering

E E E E E E

E Engineering Staff

Figure 11.1   A comparison of conventional management with MBO

While some managers are reluctant to incorporate any "participative" management system because it might erode their authority, this system permits authority to actually be strengthened by developing consent among those being directed. Since subordinates are in agreement with the superior on the objectives to be reached, a much greater commitment to accomplishment is the likely result.

Figure 11.2 compares traditional management with MBO in several key areas. While the benefits of MBO are usually evident from the start of any program designed to implement the process, they have been summarized and categorized in many different ways which tend to conform to the organization where MBO is being implemented. For an engineering department, a convenient grouping shows 15 advantages—five each for the organization, the supervisor, and the subordinate:

For the organization

    Clear goals

    Forces planning and control

    Surfaces conflicts

    Obtains commitments from supervisors

    Draws upon first-echelon expertise

For the engineering supervisor

    Forces effective delegation

    Increases time for managing

    Two-way communication

    Better evaluation criteria

    Obtains commitments from subordinates

For the subordinate

    Improves direction and guidance

    Provides autonomy

    Allows participation

    Forces feedback from above

    Improves morale

According to research conducted by Andrews and Farris on the effective management of scientists and engineers, granting substantial freedom to subordinates can act as a partial substitute for skilled supervision. However, their data show that for freedom to be effective the superior must consult with his or

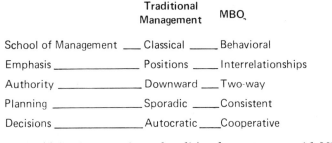

	Traditional Management	MBO
School of Management	___ Classical	_____ Behavioral
Emphasis	_____ Positions	____ Interrelationships
Authority	_____ Downward	___ Two-way
Planning	_____ Sporadic	_____ Consistent
Decisions	_____ Autocratic	___ Cooperative

Figure 11.2   A comparison of traditional management with MBO

her subordinates before making these decisions.[5] Earlier research by Pelz and Andrews suggests that freedom should be provided in an environment of direction and stimulation so that subordinates do not engage in trivial problems and stagnate.[6] The implementation of MBO by the manager can provide the type of environment where there is both freedom and a strong sense of direction. As engineers and scientists become involved in mutual goal setting with their superiors, great amounts of freedom can be granted to these subordinates to accomplish goals. A sense of direction is built into mutual goal setting but the work environment is still relatively free.

Components of MBO

Management by objectives as a system involves the following basic components. First, the establishment of clearcut objectives for the mission of the organization as a whole and the organizational units involved. Second, the establishment of objectives for each manager and subordinate that when attained will contribute to the overall objectives for the entire entrerprise. These objectives are established by a process in which the superior and the subordinate meet and jointly identify the common goals of the department, define the employee's major area of responsibility in terms of results expected, and develop or write a plan to accomplish these results. At this time, some agreement should be reached with regard to measuring criteria for evaluating performance, a specific time period for the attainment of the objective or part of it, and an agreement that at some future date a performance review session will be completed. Specifically, the objectives can be defined as what the subordinate is agreeing to accomplish in a certain period of time. Usually, this accomplishment is an end result or a performance that specifies what is to be done and how it will be measured. All objectives must be measurable. Often a department has prime objectives or overall acomplishments that the department as a whole wishes to attain over a given time period. In addition, supporting objectives exist which if accomplished will contribute to the attainment of the overall primary objectives. In this context most subordinate objectives are categorized as supporting objectives because they are narrower and contribute specifically to the attainment of primary objectives.

The third element in the MBO process is the periodic occurrence of a performance review in which the superior and the subordinate meet and discuss what has in fact been accomplished, and if failures have occurred, why they have occurred. Appraisal interviews should encompass both qualitative and quantitative aspects of a given performance in accordance with priorities that have previously been established, the difficulty of the objectives, and the extent to which deadline considerations have been met. The role of the technical manager in a performance review appraisal interview should be to act primarily as an advisor and helper rather than that of critic or judge. The discussion should be maintained in a problem-solving context with the basic objective of the interview directed toward improving performance rather than criticizing past performance. A problem-solving context will minimize defensiveness and increase the probability that constructive action will take place benefiting both the organizational unit and the individual employee.

A final component of the MBO process concerns the distribution of rewards. Each manager should endeavor to provide rewards to those employees who continually exceed or obtain their objectives as planned. However, the actual distribution of rewards such as promotion and merit salary increases should occur after the performance appraisal interview has been conducted in order to minimize individual defensiveness.

Making MBO Work in the Engineering and Scientific Environment

Once the basic elements of the MBO process are understood by the manager of the organizational unit contemplating its use, there are several steps that must be taken and pitfalls that must be avoided if the process is to be constructive. First of all, there must be a commitment to MBO from the top management team, preferably the top management of the company in which the engineering or scientific unit is located. It is not necessary that all organizational units utilize MBO—frequenty they do not—but it *is* necessary that the top management supports the efforts of the particular organizational unit in question in installing an MBO system. The authors have helped several scientific and professional organizations install MBO programs, and this experience indicates that when MBO is not supported by top management, it tends to lose its momentum after initial steps are taken to implement it, and eventually is very likely to fail. Next, it is important for the engineering or scientific division head to insure that all managers in the unit are trained on the nature, purpose, and use of MBO. This training should explain the criteria and measurement standards for a good objective, the importance of mutual goal setting, and appraisal interviewing. A good objective is stated as an end result and not as an activity. Usually a good objective begins in writing with the word *to* followed by an action verb, and specifies one key result to be obtained by a specific target date. Thus, it is measurable in terms of cost and time. Good objectives are realistic, attainable, understandable, and consistent with other organizational objectives and resources.

Ideally, when an objective is finalized, it should be put in writing to minimize conflicts of interpretation or understanding on the part of the parties involved. One of the major problems in writing objectives is that they tend to be stated in terms of an activity. For example, if a college professor were to say that his or her objective was to effectively educate students, in the context of MBO that is an activity and not an objective. It is not measurable as stated, it does not have a specific time requirement, and it says nothing about resources or parameters. Specifically, this professor could develop objectives by breaking his or her job down and indicating what constitutes effectively educating students. Key objectives could be specified in the amount of time set aside to meet with students, prepare course outlines, and by agreeing to write an article for a scholarly journal. These latter points are measurable, consistent with other organizational objectives, and stated primarily in terms of end results. Ideally, if all of these objectives were accomplished, the overall activity of effectively educating students would have a high probability of being achieved.

Each division or upper level manager of an engineering or scientific unit should develop clear-cut high level objectives for the organizational unit. These objectives should be effectively communicated to lower level managers, and their input solicited before these top level objectives are finalized. One recent study involving the use of MBO in an engineering unit found that a major problem or complaint of some middle managers was the lack of higher level management objectives.[7] Managers should also take action steps to insure that each subordinate or lower level manager in that unit understands the complexity of developing good objectives and is aware of the techniques that can be used to aid in the process.

Prior to conducting objective-setting sessions with subordinates, it is important that each manager and subordinate have substantial agreement on the duties of the job and the priorities attached to those duties. One technique that is useful in attaining this end is for each party involved to prepare separate lists of important job tasks in a prioritized order. Next, the superior and subordinate should discuss the listing to see what areas of disagreement or agreement exist. In this way they are in an excellent position to reach a congruent relationship with regard to job responsibilities and duties. Once this congruence is attained, the manager and the subordinate are ready to establish goals together. It is essential that "mutuality" occurs, namely, the manager must be flexible enough to modify some objectives on the basis of subordinate input. Wihtout mutuality, the subordinate feels that he or she is being dictated to, and many of the problems associated with autocracy and loss of autonomy and responsibility emerge.

A major obstacle is that many managers regard MBO as simply a numbers game, and tend to place excessive emphasis on quantity rather than quality. Appropriate use of communication feedback from subordinates can be effective in counteracting this difficulty. Additionally, agreement with the subordinate on job content and priorities can help to eliminate overlapping responsibilities between departments and individuals. Managers must be willing to delegate, and they must encourage subordinates to assume responsibility. Effective delegation in management by objectives also minimizes paperwork, which is often seen as an obstacle to adopting MBO. Any supportive activities that the managerial staff can assume which minimizes the paperwork for lower level managers and subordinates will encourage the MBO process to be fruitful for the entire unit.

The manager of a research and development unit faces a particularly tough problem in the successful formulation and development of objectives with subordinates. Typically, no agreement exists with regard to the measurement of scientific performance. Moreover, an examination of the studies on measurement of scientific performance reveals little agreement among investigators as to what constitutes scientific output or what measures should be used to reflect it.[8] Among the more commonly used measures is to apply a variety of techniques to measure the quantity and quality of written output. The ability of the researcher to meet given time constraints is also regarded as important. Whether MBO is used or not, many authorities on research and development management agree that attempts to establish objectives for research units is a useful and often necessary managerial task.

While it is difficult to establish clear-cut performance objectives for the scientist engaged in pure research, or for other professionals who are simply exploring problems or essentially dealing with the unknown, some current tools may be useful in the appraisal process. For example, one approach which can help to alleviate this problem is for the manager to work with subordinates in the development of *behaviorally anchored rating scales.* This performance appraisal tool involves the development of scaled statements that describe effective and ineffective specific job behaviors associated with getting results. These behaviors can be constructed by categorizing and systematically scaling a manager's reports of critical incidents of effective of ineffective job performance. When specific behaviors are identified, it is assumed that a distinction can be made between more effective and less effective ways of doing the job.

William Kearney provides specific guidelines on how to construct behaviorally anchored rating scales as follows:[9]

1. Supervisors and subordinates identify activities critical to effective job performance, namely, performance dimensions.

2. Specific statements based on observations of both effective and ineffective job performance are drawn from these dimensions. Attention is given to job actions that reflect very favorable or unfavorable performance.

3. These statements are then assigned by the manager or job holder to the appropriate dimension. Mutual agreement among participants is important in making this assignment.

4. These statements are then scaled from 1 to 9 on an effective-ineffective continuum.

Performance can then be measured against these dimensions as part of MBO or part of basic performance appraisal. While this approach can be helpful to all managers, it is particularly useful to technical managers where end results (goals) are had to quantify. A simplified behaviorally anchored rating scale for a design engineer is shown in Figure 11.3.

Once objectives are established through a process of mutual agreement with subordinates and specific time periods for attainment of these objectives are accepted by subordinates, performance interviews should be conducted at the appropriate times. For technical personnel, the time period is usually once each year.

The application of effective communication skills as developed in Chapter 7 is particularly helpful to conducting constructive appraisal interviews. Technical managers should focus on the problem, direct the communication at improving performance, appear to be interested, and offer constructive and helpful suggestions to the subordinate.

In the early stages of making MBO work, there may be some periods of disenchantment with the process. Since MBO involves some new processes in interviewing and objective development that have not been used before, managers and subordinates become uncertain about the necessity or usefulness of these extra efforts. This disenchantment is normal. Some managers and subordinates feel threatened by agreeing to accomplish end results in specific time periods. This type of threat or pressure can be minimized by mutual goal setting where the concerns of the subordinate are fully shared and supported at the goal-setting sessions. If good performers are clearly rewarded by the management, the entire engineering or scientific group will see that it is advantageous to both set goals and accomplish them.

It is useful in the initial stages of management by objectives to move rather slowly and build on past successes, because an attempt to move quickly can overwhelm subordinates. Extra paperwork, interview time, and attempting to establish a complete set of objectives can be so threatening to subordinates that

156

Rating scale	Knowledge and work output
Extremely good performance	This engineer has current, in-depth knowledge for his or her specialization and always correctly identifies and solves technical problems in a timely fashion. This engineer also has excellent communication skills and consistently interfaces well with superiors, subordinates, and other technical and nontechnical persons.
Neither good nor poor performance	This engineer exhibits reasonable ability to solve problems. He or she may require the assistance of others to complete more difficult work assignments. His or her work product must be carefully checked. From time to time certain assignments must be redone.
Extremely poor performance	This engineer is operating with below-normal technical ability. He or she requires considerable assistance to complete assignments. Much of the work output is unacceptable. This person spends considerable time discussing nonproductive issues and does not meet time/schedule deadlines. If this person is not a relative of the boss, he or she exhibits high mental anxiety concerning loss of employment.

Figure 11.3   Simplified behaviorially anchored rating scale for a design engineer

the system fails because of the lack of cooperation. The total organizational unit must work together to make MBO work. Thus, upper level managers must provide an environment where threats are minimized and the action is taken at a pace that subordinates can adjust to.

Conclusion

Management by objectives is not a panacea, but it can be a very useful tool in improving managerial effectiveness in the engineering and scientific environment. While it is not easily applied, there is considerable evidence to suggest that technical organizations can benefit from a well-planned and functioning management by objectives program.

Notes

1. For an original discussion of the MBO concept, see Peter F. Drucker, *The Practice of Management*, Harper & Row, New York, 1954; and George S. Odiorne, *Management by Objectives*, Pitman, New York, 1965.

2. Timothy T. Serey and Desmond D. Martin, "The Impact of Selected Management Tools on Organizational Effectiveness," College of Business Administration, University of Cincinnati, Cincinnati, Ohio, April 1979 (mimeographed).

3. Jacob B. Paperman and Desmond D. Martin, Human Resource Accounting: A Managerial Tool? *Personnel*, March-April 1977, pp. 41-50.

4. Robert H. Mills, How Job Conflict and Ambiguity Affect R. & D. Professionals, *Research Management*, vol. XVIII, no. 4, July 1975.

5. Frank M. Andrews and George F. Farris, Supervisory Practices and Innovation in Scientific Teams. *Personnel Psychology*, vol. 20, no. 4, Winter 1967.

6. D. C. Pelz and F. M. Andrews, Autonomy, Coordination, and Stimulation in Relation to Scientific Achievement. *Behavioral Science*, vol. XI, 1966, pp. 89-97.

7. Joseph P. Martino, Managing Engineers by Objectives. *IEEE Transactions on Engineering Management*, vol. EM23, no. 4, November 1976, pp. 168-174.

8. S. A. Edwards and M. W. McCarrey, Measuring the Performance of Researchers. *Research Management*, January 1973, pp. 34-40.

9. W. J. Kearney, Behaviorally Anchored Rating Scales—MBO's Missing Ingredient. *Personnel Journal*, January 1979, pp. 20-25.

12 Managerial and
Organizational Effectiveness

Basic Components of Organizational Effectiveness

As indicated previously, the purpose of this book is to provide engineering, scientific, and professional staff managers with tested management and behavioral concepts and techniques that can be applied to increase both managerial and organizational effectiveness. The authors believe that a significant proportion of an organization's effectiveness can be measured by the quality of its performance in five specific areas:

Productivity (a ratio of input to output)

The presence of clearly stated goals

Adaptability and flexibility

The quality and effectiveness of intra- and interorganizational communication

The choice of an appropriate management style

Effectiveness Begins with Good Planning

In order to do well in these areas, the technical manager must plan and organize well. The basic elements in good long- and short-range planning were discussed in Chapter 2. It is important to note that throughout this book stress has been placed on the significance of separating planning from doing and the facilitative role of the manager. Short- and long-range plans should be based on clearly understood and stated goals for both the unit being managed and the overall organization. Specific plans should be established that help to remove obstacles to goal accomplishment among subordinates.

As developed in Chapter 6, individuals have differing and often unique needs that warrant special consideration in good managerial planning. Participative management can be extremely helpful in both discerning the nature of these needs and responding to them. In giving consideration to individual needs, managers should remember that equity is a vital part of effective planning. A given subordinate's perception of equity or inequity is usually judged only in relation to how other people are being treated in the same situation. Plans should attempt to establish predictable relationships for subordinates once they understand the situation. Individual differences can be accounted for in the context of different situations without upsetting equity. For example, a manager's plan to transfer employees among jobs can differentiate among subordinates on the basis of skills, health, or special interests as long as these criteria are clearly understood by the subordinates involved. Thus, effective communication is vital to successful planning.

Technical managers should plan for both contingencies and conflict among subordinates. A certain amount of conflict is both normal and healthy, and it is unrealistic to have a goal of creating a managerial environment that is totally free of conflict. But in recent years it has become increasingly important to establish some kind of procedural due process which will enable employees to communicate concerns about inequitable treatment. For such a system to work, all employees must have the right to use it, and provision for a third, impartial party to hear unresolved cases is necessary. While these elements have been common parts of collective bargaining agreements for many years, they are only recently being used in nonunionized settings. Since high perceived equity among subordinates improves levels of cooperation with both peers and managers and tends to increase motivation, managerial attention to both equity and due process in the planning process will usually yield high payoffs.

Organizatonal Structure: A Major Tool of Effectiveness

As suggested in Chapter 3, good organizing and structuring is essential for efficiency and effectiveness. In fact, the quality of a given technical manager's organizational structure has a lot to do with the level of employee adaptability and flexibility which is attained. Needless to say, adaptability and flexibility are particularly crucial to technical environments because these environments are subject to rapid and often unpredictable change. Good organization should enable the engineering or scientific unit to respond effectively to environmental requirements and facilitate the realization of employee potential.

In order to develop good organization, managerial knowledge of principles, alternative structures, and the elements of sound line-staff relationships as developed in Chapter 3 is essential. It is often useful to define and group tasks, and allocate assignments based on employee preferences whenever possible and practical. The modern technical manager should be aware that a specific technique called MAPS (multivariate analysis, participation, and structure) has been proposed as an aid to integrating goal-setting behavior and organizational structure and is getting increasing attention in the management literature. Ralph Kilman concludes from his studies on the use of the MAPS method that the evidence to date indicates that MAPS generates sufficient confidence from its applications that its ethical use can be supported.[1] While it is beyond the scope of this book to deal in detail with this rather complex tool, a brief discussion will follow concering its applicability and usefulness.[2] The MAPS method considers both the nature of the tasks to be accomplished and the preferences or interests of specific employees in performing this work.[3] This technique is similar to management by objectives in that organizational members interact with their managers in objective setting and task identification. Mutlivariate analysis is then used to cluster interrelated tasks. Once preferences for given task clusters are known, multivariate statistical techniques can be used to assign employees to the organizational subunits that best fit their interests and preferences.[4] In view of the high needs for autonomy and strong preferences for specific task assignments associated with engineers and scientists, the MAPS method seems to offer potential help to the technical manager who is trying to build an effective organizational structure.

While attention was given in Chapter 3 to selection of new personnel, managers more commonly face the problem of allocation and assignment of work among existing personnel on a periodic basis. The MAPS method offers potential help in this latter problem as well as in the assignment of tasks to new employees. It also provides a framework for looking at the two critical variables in good structuring, namely, tasks and people.

Many prominent management authorities including Drucker suggest that a decision should be made at the lowest level in the organization that is closest to the scene of action.[5] Minimizing the number of organizational levels tends to lower the levels where decisions are made, and also simplifies the organizational structure. Simple structures are easier to understand and foster more effective communication than complex ones. Consequently, as long as the given structure will do the job, keep it as simple as possible.[6]

Changing Attitudes and Values of American Workers

Changing values and attitudes precipitated by cultural change have added to the complexity of the managerial task in recent years. A government-sponsored study in 1973 indicates that worker attitudes toward welfare and leisure have undergone significant change.[7] For example, earlier studies concluded that most workers associated hard work with both getting ahead and raising self-esteem, but current research indicates that employees in increasing numbers no longer subscribe to this belief.[8] Accepting welfare is no longer considered demeaning by many people, and hard work is not seen as leading directly to advancement. As pointed out in Chapter 9, rewards must be tied to performance, but many managers continue to relate individual performance appraisal to vague traits or seniority rather than to actual goal-related accomplishment. Recent trends in the use of MBO-related performance appraisal systems including behaviorally anchored rating scales offer some encouragement as a potential solution to this problem (see Chapter 11). Employees who realize that personal reward is attained through good job performance are more likely to contribute to organizational effectiveness.

New Credentials Requirements

Unfortunately, in many instances credentials needed to qualify for employment have been increased by management, but job content has remained relatively unchanged. Jobs that required only a high school diploma or less in 1950 now require a college degree as a basic educational qualification.[9] Since the job content is no more challenging, many employees become frustrated with their job assignments. Many, but not all, engineering, scientific, and professional organizations are no exception to this problem. A number of jobs in these organizations currently exist that require a technical degree which could be performed by a nondegree technician without difficulty, but there must be a careful balance. Products that were designed by draftsmen years ago should now be designed by engineers who can calculate mechanical stresses and electrical gradient, or solve other basic engineering problems in order to avoid product failure. Technical managers should upgrade jobs where possible, and be aware of the impact of the rising educational level of the work force on job satisfaction and motivation.

An Educated Work Force Is Not Automatically More Productive

High levels of educational attainment have also generated a more mobile work force which has reduced the importance of company loyalty to many employees. The practical managerial implication of reduced loyalty is that managers who do not continually strive to make their work unit environment responsive to employee needs may find that they are losing their most valuable employees to competing organizations. Years of service or other factors relating to a given employee's history with the company may turn out to be quite irrelevant.

While techniques for building the right work environment have been given special attention throughout the second·half of this book, it is important to remember that increasing amounts of time pressure and minimum control over one's job activities are major problems to top quality engineering and scientific personnel. In fact, Martin Patchen's comprehensive study of the Tennessee Valley Authority, which employs many engineering personnel, found that these employees attach great importance to control over work methods and a work environment that is characterized by low amounts of time pressure.[10] As time limits are increased, employees tend to take less pride in their work; namely, they hurry to complete the assigned tasks and concentrate less on how well tasks are done.[11] Today's educated employees regard reduced time pressure, autonomy, control over work methods, and communication feedback on performance as essential elements of a good working environment. Each of these elements can be considered a proper component of an enriched job. It is good managerial practice for the technical manager to analyze both current job design and managerial practices for the specific units that fall within his or her realm of accountability. Although a first glance or reading of the above analysis may lead one to conclude that reduced time pressure will result in more free time for workers to engage in nonproductive tasks, statistical evidence does not support that conclusion. In general, reduced time pressure leads to greater productivity in sustained (long-run) managerial relationships with employees.

Career Development in the Professional Organization

Aspiring young employees such as today's new engineer or scientist are vitally interested in personal professional growth and career advancement. One recent study of 277 municipal employees examined the relationship between the extent of career planning and certian career effectiveness variables such as salary, career involvement, and adaptability. This study's findings suggest that extensive career planning is related to higher salaries, more career involvement, and adaptability.[12] One career planning model asserts that the establishment of career goals by employees leads to increased efforts to achieve these goals, which results in more career involvement. If these goals are successfully attained, employee performance and self-esteem are increased.[13] Thus, there is growing evidence that specific attention to career planning is important both to the manager and the employee. Although advising young people on how to manage their careers is difficult, technical managers are often confronted with this task.

Some of the useful advice that these managers can offer new subordinates and may find applicable to their own situation, especially if they are new managers, is contained in the following list, which is adapted from the separate work of Webber, Jennings, and Buskirk.[14]

1. Make an accurate self-appraisal of the real criteria that are being used in evaluating your performance. Try to accurately appraise your own performance against these criteria, and concentrate your time and effort in improving perceived performance deficiencies in these critical areas.

2. Keep yourself up-to-date in your field. This process includes continually reading current literature, and being aware of seminars and presentations on new and important topics.

3. Strive to be an active influence in organizational decisions, and try to gain positions with high visibility where your performance can be observed by higher officials.

4. Develop good relationships with superiors that are regarded highly by the organizational hierarchy.

5. Seize opportunities by nominating yourself for positions that involve advancement. On the other hand, do not be afraid to turn down a promotion for which you are not qualified, or a job in which you assess that your chances for success are very low.

6. A managerial position involves a series of dependency relationships. If you find these relationships repulsive, you may not be cut out to be a manager.

7. Written job descriptions are often either too narrow, outdated, or both, so do not be afraid to move out beyond the job description in performing your duties. In fact, many times successful job performance requires such action.

Importance of the First Job Assignment

The characteristics of the first job assignment are important to the technical manager, employee, and organization. Employee turnover is often highest during the first year or so of employment among qualified employees, and proper handling of early assignments by superiors will often reduce turnover among more valued new employees.

Managers should realize that the first career assignment is a time of great apprehension for the new recruit. He or she may feel that this assignment is the real test of the value of acquired technical skills in an engineering or scientific educational program, and failure at this job will mean that the value of their educational investment in time and money is subject to question. Needless to say, this possiblity represents a strong potential threat to both the satisfaction and self-esteem of the new employee. Thus, technical managers should recognize these apprehensions and offer support to new engineers during their critical first year.

Since many organizations regard first-year assignments as relatively unimportant probationary periods for new employees, technical managers may not have the upper management support in their special handing of the new recruit. For example, some organizations do not make important job assignments to employees with less than 1 year of service; consequently, new employees' fears of failure during the first year may be exaggerated. The technical manager who understands these differences between the overall managerial perceptions versus the new employee's perceptions of the significance of first-year assignments can be helpful in increasing organizational effectiveness.

Avoiding Professional Obsolescence

While the period of time involved in which professional obsolescence will occur varies by organization and technological type, it is generally agreed that unless new knowledge is continually made available to technical employees, they will become obsolete. Many firms learn from experience that highly educated employees become a liability to the firm unless new learning which is equivalent to their current state of knowledge is generated in 12 to 18 years from their date of initial employment. Specifically, if an engineer enters an organization with a Ph.D. in 1981, by 1995 he or she should acquire new knowledge equal to what they acquired in pursuit of the doctorate. For example, engineers who earned doctorates in the late 1940s did not have courses in solid state physics because such courses did not exist, yet in the late fifties and early sixties solid state technology became an integral part of the technological base of many firms. These facts underscore the importance of technical and skill training in the engineering and scientific environment, and a supportive personnel department can be very helpful in coordinating training programs. Each program should be tailored to the specific needs of the given firm, and training planners and directors should avoid the two common pitfalls of copying programs from other firms or spoon feeding participants.

A climate that creates a desire to learn should be provided by the technical manager. Two essential ingredients of this environment are first, specific rewards for successful completion of training programs given to participants (e.g., opportunities for advancement and assignment of more challenging work); and second, recognizing employees who improve or do outstanding work on their current jobs. These factors are generally consistent with modern approaches to motivation (see Chapter 8).

The issue of the dual career is also related to the professional obsolescence problem. Does the engineer who becomes a manager devote virtually all of his or her time to managerial problems and spend little or no time on new developments in the field? The logical answer to this question is no, because keeping up-to-date in the field is an important part of the managerial task. An ideal managerial climate continues to reward those managers for outstanding technical work, and encourages individual managers to attend seminars and other presentations that relate to the development of their technical knowledge. While the technical manager's time for professional development activity is limited, some time should be carefully allocated to this process. Good time management practices are essential, and the modern technical manager can get some pointers from the discussion of efficient time management later in this chapter.

Job Enrichment and Time Management

Is Job Enrichment the Answer?

Modifications in managerial practices should be considered when current practices seem to be resulting in increased time pressure, reduced autonomy, and little performance feedback. Job redesign (enrichment) should be considered when there is little challenge or intrinsic satisfaction associated with the specific task assignments, and when employees are permitted little control over work methods.

While job enrichment is at least a partial answer to dealing with the rising educational level of todays worker, enrichment programs often involve significant dollar costs to the organization. A recent study by Antone Alber which was based on information obtained from 189 companies and six government agencies found that five major costs were commonly associated with job enrichment.[15] These costs included pressure for increased wages and salaries by "enriched" workers with new modified job duties. When jobs were modified and made more complex, more floor area or storage space was needed in several instances. This additional space could be transferred into increased cost of facilities. Also, inventory costs may rise because larger parts inventories are needed to accommodate differing processes.[16] Training and implementation costs can rise as special or new training is needed for the existing supervisory or trained staff, and some firms reported that outside consultants were hired to assist with new training needs.[17]

It must be emphasized, however, that the nature of many engineering and scientific job assignments makes them conducive to job enrichment; consequently, many of these enrichment costs will be lower in engineering and scientific units. Nevertheless, each technical manager should be aware of these increased costs and approach job enrichment decisions with adequate time and caution. The decision-making process outlined in Chapter 5 can be useful in organizing these kinds of decisions. Since many firms in the Alber study experienced several benefits from their job enrichment efforts, this decision can be difficult. In fact, increased production in both quality and quantity as well as more job satisfaction was related to job enrichment in a large number of the firms in the Alber survey.[18] Some of these firms also experienced a reduction in employee turnover and absenteeism. Thus, as is the case with most complex managerial decisions, the technical manager must weigh the potential costs of enriching jobs against the probable benefits in order to determine the impact of a job enrichment program on organizational effectiveness.

Emerging environmental factors mean that modern engineering, scientific, and professional staff managers are constantly faced with decisions that are associated with considerable amounts of stress, and job enrichment decisions also fit into this category. Psychological stress has a definite impact on the decision-making process. Janis and Mann define a "stressful" event as any change in the environment that is likely to induce a high degree of unpleasant emotion such as anxiety or guilt.[19] These authors also indicate that several functional relationships exist between psychological stress and decisional conflict as discussed below.[20]

When a decision maker expects a given decision to leave many important needs and goals unfulfilled, stress is high. If a decision maker is firmly entrenched in a present course of action, but faces new, attractive alternatives to this existing situation, stress tends to be high. Stress is also high when a decision maker faces a threat of serious loss and perceived time to take steps to avoid such loss is too short to properly evaluate each possible alternative.

According to Janis and Mann, high stress situations are likely to result in faulty information processing which lowers the quality of the decision.[21] Conversely, in low stress situations, the decision maker may not give adequate thought and attention to the possible alternatives. Specifically, one or more of the important decision-making steps of systems analysis as developed in Chapter 5 may be neglected.

Human relations knowledge and skills are more important now than at any time in the past in order to be effective and to derive personal satisfaction from the managerial job. Identifying and relating to subordinate needs is often the cornerstone of increasing the value of the organization's human assets. Elements of the traditional approach to managing engineers and scientists that tended to treat these employees as malleable factors in the production process who could be molded easily into a productive segment of the organization is both outdated and impractical. In spite of the complexities of human behavior in the organizational environment, generally, and in the technical and creative environment, specifically, managers must continually strive to understand individual behavior.

It is clear that while much more is still to be understood about behavior, a great deal is already known. Technical managers who devote considerable time and effort to learning more about management and behavior will have a distinct advantage over their counterparts who are unwilling to make this investment. In fact, an investment in improving skills in both directing and understanding people may be both useful and necessary in today's complex and competitive management setting.

More Emphasis on Time Management

The increasing cost of executive talent is going to result in continued emphasis on effective time management. While managing time successfully is a complex process which relates to the unique makeup and needs of individuals as developed in Chapter 6, there are some basic steps that technical managers can take that will result in more efficient time utilization. Some of these important steps are outlined below:[22]

1. Establish clear-cut goals for yourself and your unit.

2. Set time priorities in accordance with these goals. It is important to focus first on doing the right things, and then attempt to do them properly. Many organizational and personal problems have surfaced because the wrong things were done. For example, some technical managers fail to get promoted because although they are efficient, they are not concentrating their efforts on important high priority activities.

3. A pro-active or planning stance is preferred to a reactive or "fire-fighting" stance. Pro-active planning gives a manager better control of potential problem situations.

4. In both setting priorities and in being pro-active, it is often necessary to refuse some specific requests for help by both superiors and subordinates. Managers who have a strong desire to be liked often have difficulty saying "no" to others. This tendency can easily result in the inefficient use of time, because a large amount of time is consumed on low priority or inappropriate activities.

5. Good time management involves a willingness to delegate authority to subordinates. Thus, another argument for delegation is added to a list that has grown steadily throughout this book.

6. Finally, a daily time log which accounts for where you spend your time can be helpful in solving personal time management problems.[23] This completed log is most useful if it is matched with preestablished goals, so that the amount of time spent on low priority items can be identified. For example, low priority meetings and phone conservations are among the biggest time wasters.

Future Trends in Technical Management

Overview and Problem Identification

Engineers and technical people who will be managing organizations during the late twentieth century and into the next century will be facing a number of problems in a difficult environment. The fundamental challenges for engineers in management will center on a sound grasp of the relevant technology, communication skills, and a capacity for effectively dealing with and motivating people.[24] While the effective manager today requires these skills and abilities, the need for communication, technology understanding, and human interface skills is predicted to increase for the successful technical manager of the future.

The major problems confronting future technical managers may be grouped into seven categories as outlined below:

Energy availability and cost

Lagging productivity

Economic difficulties

Social concern and reform

Environmental requirements

Government regulation and controls

Product liability

Energy Availability and Cost

Is there an energy crisis? The answer is obviously *yes*. The number one problem of technical managers of the future will be obtaining necessary energy for business operations at an affordable cost. While the world may not yet have an energy shortage, there is a crisis. Part of the crisis is that at times certain energy demands exceed available supplies, and we are rapidly moving toward the point where total demand *will* exceed supply. Perhaps the most serious aspect in the short term is a deepening monetary crisis. During recent years, the U.S. balance of payments has had a significant imbalance because of the monies expended for imported oil. If this trend continues, the U.S. economy is in jeopardy. Indeed, the world monetary system could collapse.

The Problem of Lagging Productivity

The U.S. Bureau of the Budget has provided a general definition of productivity as follows: "Productivity estimates compare the amount of resources used with the volume of products or services produced."[25] In manufacturing industries the common measure of productivity relates unit of product output to labor-hours input.

Productivity in the private economy grew over the post-World War II period at an approximate annual rate of 3.1 percent. This average rate of increase is for the period from 1946 through 1974. Examination of the data reveals a slightly higher rate of 3.6 percent in the earlier postwar period. This dropped to 3.0 percent during the early 1960s, and in the 1970s dropped to 2.4 percent. Overall, the rate of growth has tended to decline somewhat during the last few decades. In recent years, productivity gains have been very small.[26]

Following an analysis of productivity in the manufacturing sector, Malstrom and Shell predicted that "by the year 2000, manufacturing productivity levels will have leveled off or declined to new lower levels that remain relatively constant from period to period!"[27] If this should happen, the overall quality of life in the United States would suffer.

Productivity growth is an essential factor in the continued economic well being of the United States. One of the primary benefits is increased worker income. Real compensation to the worker has risen at about the same rate as labor productivity. In addition, the consumer benefits through increased goods and services at affordable costs. Prices usually rise the least in those areas where productivity is rising and the most where productivity is lagging. Achieving improved productivity is important in determining the growth of real earnings and our standard of living. In the long run, productivity improvements may be the principal way to offset the impact of drastic increases in the prices of energy and basic raw materials.[28] The problem of lagging productivity is a major problem for the technical manager of the future.

Economic Difficulties

Present economic difficulties as well as future problems in this areas are closely related to the previously mentioned issues of energy and productivity. The continued wage-price spiral usually held responsible for the inertia of the inflationary process will be a continued problem for management in the future. It is clear that the cost of technical operations will continue to climb. For example, for a unit of output such as a new product, the required research and development activities will cost more in the future. The position of the United States in the world marketplace is highly dependent on the success of technical innovation. Consequently, the need for effective management to realize maximum output from the technical work force is critical.

Social Concern and Reform

Social concern and reform has impacted the modern worker. In recent years the work force has taken on a different profile. As previously discussed in this chapter, workers are better educated, and they have greater social awareness than the generation that preceded them. Typical worker concerns include underemployment, unemployment, and the need for environmental improvements.

Social concern and reform is also creeping into business. Not since the days of Franklin D. Roosevelt and the New Deal has the field of corporate governance been so active in generating proposals of reform. As Warren Bennis recently put it, "everybody's in the act, it seems—not just Ralph Nader, who nags, hassles, and litigates on behalf of corporate social responsibility or the ubiquitous Lewis D. Gilbert, who presses for reform and sues corporations to make them more responsible to the shareholder."[29]

The social concern and reform trends are likely to continue for individuals and corporations. Consequently, the technical manager of the future must be able to integrate these complex changing views into his or her leadership role.

Environmental Requirements

Environmental requirements will continue to be a major concern of technical managers, as previously mentioned, in part because of the changing social views of many individuals and corporations. Requirements for improved air quality, wastewater treatment, and solid/hazardous waste disposal will continue to intensify, and will be factors to consider in many management decisions concerning new products, processes, and physical facilities.

One of the problems associated with environmental improvements is that most of the required equipment is not cost effective in the short run. That is, while most plant modifications leading to environmental improvements require substantial capital investment, they do not provide any greater productive output. The technical manager of the future will focus on attaining the proper balance of "return on investment" and environmental conformance.

Government Regulation and Control

Government regulations and controls are projected to increase over the next several years, especially in the areas of environmental concerns, consumer product safety, and worker health and safety. Government agencies such as the Environmental Protection Agency and the Occupational Safety and Health Administration will continue to impose greater restrictions and requirements on most industries, both product manufacturing and service organizations. The technical manager of the future must be able to effectively and efficiently meet these requirements.

Product Liability

Product liability is a "sleeping giant" type of problem. There has been a proliferation of product liability suits across the United States during the past several years following the adoption of the law of strict liability in tort. Product liability suits have covered a wide range of alleged inferior product designs and defective product manufacturing cases. In addition to corporations being named, managers and project engineers have also been personally cited in a number of recent suits. It is predicted that the ultimate threat product liability poses to industry will surpass the threat posed to the medical profession by malpractice.

The rationale for product liability is acceptable to all persons. Certainly if someone is injured by a defective product, then the product's designer/manufacturer should be held accountable. However, the prevailing interpretations of the law and the resulting cases against many manufacturers leave many unanswered questions and unexplained outcomes. If this problem is not fairly resolved with major legislation changes, the difficulties for technical managers in the future will be monumental.

Conclusions and Implications

In summary, the years ahead will be increasingly problem laden and more complex from a management point of view. The successful technical manager will be able to transform these problems into opporutnities. The need for developing effective management skills and abilities will continue at an increased level. In addition to the insight and ability to change problems into opportunities, the technical manager of tomorrow must be able to accomplish more with less resources. In some ways it seems the future is now!

Notes

1. For a detailed discussion on MAPS design technology, see Ralph H. Kilman, On Integrating Knowledge Utilization with Knowledge Development: The Philosophy Behind the MAPS Design Technology. *Academy of Management Review,* July 1979, pp. 417-426.

2. *Ibid.*

3. Ralph H. Kilman, An Organic Adaptive Organization: The MAPS Method. *Personnel,* May-June 1974, pp. 35-47.

4. *Ibid.*

5. Peter F. Drucker, *Management Tasks, Responsibilities, Practices,* Harper & Row, New York, 1973, p. 545.

6. *Ibid.*

7. Report of a Special Task Force to the Secretary of Health, Education, and Welfare, *Work in America,* The MIT Press, Cambridge, Mass., 1973, p. 10.

8. *Ibid,* p. 11.

9. *Ibid,* p. 138.

10. Martin Patchen, *Participation, Achievement, and Involvement on the Job,* Prentice-Hall, Englewood Cliffs, N.J., 1970, p. 234.

11. *Ibid,* p. 235.

12. Sam Gould, Characteristics of Career Planners in Upwardly Mobile Occupations. *Academy of Management Journal,* September 1979, pp. 539-550.

13. *Ibid.*

14. For an excellent discussion of career advice, see Ross A. Weber, Career Problems of Young Managers. *California Management Review,* vol. 18, no. 4, 1976, pp. 19-33. See also E. E. Jennings, *Routes to the Executive Suite,* McGraw-Hill, New York, 1971; and R. H. Buskirk, *Your Career: How to Plan It, Manage It, Change It,* Cahnero, Boston, 1976.

15. Antone F. Alber, The Real Cost of Job Enrichment. *Business Horizons,* vol. 22, no. 1, February 1979, pp. 60-72.

16. *Ibid.*

17. *Ibid.*

18. *Ibid.*

19. Irving L. Janis and Leon Mann, *Decision Making: A Psychological Analysis of Conflict, Choice and Commitment,* The Free Press, New York, 1977, p. 50.

20. *Ibid.*

21. *Ibid.,* p. 52.

22. Several of these ideas are adapted from Richard A. Moreno, Executive Time Management I: Organizational Support for Better Time Management. *Advanced Management Journal,* Winter 1978, pp. 36-40.

23. Borden Coulter and Georgy Hayo, Executive Time Management II. How to Budget Your time. *Advanced Management Journal,* Winter 1978, pp. 41-48.

24. J. T. Kane, Technical Communications and People-Related Skills Seen as Basis for Engineering Management. *Professional Engineer,* vol. 49, no. 2, February 1979, pp. 16-17.

25. *Measuring Productivity of Federal Government Organizations,* U.S. Bureau of the Budget, Government Printing Office, 1964.

26. R. L. Shell and E. M. Malstrom, "Measurement and Enhancement of Work Force Productivity in Service Organizations," *Proceedings, Twenty-Fifth Annual Joint Engineering Management Conference,* 1977, pp. 29-35.

27. E. M. Malstrom and R. L. Shell, Projections for Future Manufacturing Work Force Productivity, *Proceedings, Twenty-Fith Annual Joint Engineering Management Conference,* 1977, pp. 41-47.

28. R. L. Shell and E. M. Malstrom, Measurement and Enhancement of Work Force Productivity in Service Organizations, *Proceedings, Twenty-Fifth Annual Joint Engineering Management Conference,* 1977, pp. 29-35.

29. W. G. Bennis, RX for Corporate Boards, *Technology Review,* vol. 81, no. 3, December 1978-January 1979, p. 12.

Index

D